Critical Pedagogy
Notes from the Real World

SECOND EDITION

WITHDRAWN

Joan Wink

California State University, Stanislaus

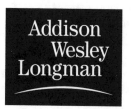

Addison
Wesley
Longman

An imprint of Addison Wesley Longman, Inc.

New York • Reading, Massachusetts • Menlo Park, California • Harlow, England
Don Mills, Ontario • Sydney • Mexico City • Madrid • Amsterdam

Dedication

For Bop-Bop, Wyatt, and Luke and the Prarie People who love them.

Editor-in-Chief: Priscilla McGeehon
Marketing Manager: Renée Ortbals
Full Service Production Manager: Mark Naccarelli
Project Coordination and Text Design: Nesbitt Graphics, Inc.
Electronic Page Makeup: Nesbitt Graphics, Inc.
Cover Design Manager: Nancy Danahy
Cover Designer: Keithley & Associates, Inc.
Senior Print Buyer: Hugh Crawford
Printer and Binder: The Maple-Vail Book Manufacturing Group
Cover Printer: Coral Graphic Services

For permission to use copyrighted material, grateful acknowledgement is made to the copyright holders on page 190, which is hereby made part of this copyright page.

Library of Congress Cataloging-in-Publication Data
Wink, Joan.
    Critical pedagogy: notes from the real world/Joan Wink.—2nd ed.
        p.   cm.
    Includes bibliographical references (p. 0) and index.
    ISBN 0-8013-3257-5
    1. Critical pedagogy—United States.   I. Title.
    370. 11'5—dc21   99-24790
                                                                CIP

Copyright © 2000 by Addison-Wesley Longman Inc.

Please visit our website at http://www.awlonline.com

0-8013-3257-5

78910–MA–04 03

Contents

WITHDRAWN

chapter 2

chapter 3

chapter 4

Critical Pedagogy: How in the World Do You Do It?   119

chapter **5**

Preface

"Did you write a cookbook?" he excitedly asked me when he saw my book on the kitchen counter. He is the local farrier, a person who shoes horses.

"No." I replied.

"Is it about ballistics?" a second man asked me. He is the fertilizer person.

"No," I replied.

"If it's not about bullets, I won't buy it," he emphatically told me. "I am doing research with the local university. You know how those university professors are," he explained. "They only want the prestige of discovering something radically different about ballistics. I want a better bullet."

"Hmmm, maybe bullets are more important than schools," I replied.

"That's what capitalism is all about," the fertilizer man explained for me.

So, if this is not a cookbook, nor a bullets book, what in the world is it? This is a book about my own critical reflections on 30 years of pedagogy, which is the interaction between teaching and learning. Sometimes I reflect critically on what I hear in the classroom and community, and sometimes I reflect critically on what I hear in my kitchen. These human interactions often lead me to relearn and even unlearn some of my long-held assumptions. Critical pedagogy opens the door to a broader and deeper perspective on teaching and learning in the classroom and the community.

THE PURPOSE

My purpose is to think new thoughts that are applicable to critical teaching and learning for the twenty-first century. I do not teach the way I taught in 1966, my first year of teaching; I do not learn the way I learned in 1966; I do not believe the way I believed in 1966; I do not know in the way I knew in 1966. My ways of knowing come from my experiences with living, learning, and teaching since that time.

If I were to describe my ways of knowing, I suspect I would say they are holistic (I want to see the whole puzzle first); gender-based (being a wife, a mom, and a grammie has taught me more than I can yet understand); linguistic (I love languages); and pluralistic (the "other" anything fascinates me). There you have it—the mystery is gone. The professional and personal are so interwoven in my experiences, that I no longer try to pretend they are separate. I did not think that way either in 1966.

In this book, we will see teaching and learning through the lens of critical pedagogy. When I began teaching, I saw schools through the lens of behaviorism. I no longer see that way. When you are finished with this book, I do not expect you to think, to know, and to see the way I do. I would hope that you have reflected critically on your own theory and practice and understand your own perspective better.

I do not want every page of this book to be affirming to all. I do want to prod and to poke a tad; I want you to think and to rethink and to unthink. I want you to relate your new thoughts to the context of your life and your experiences.

THE AUDIENCE FOR THIS BOOK

This book is for people who care about schools. All are welcome to the dialogue on critical pedagogy.

HOW TO READ THIS BOOK

The first edition was arranged sequentially; this one, less so. I think you can pick it up and read anywhere, based on how much time you have.

DISTINGUISHING CHARACTERISTICS

Throughout the book, I will tell stories. Many of the stories I have lived. Other stories have been told to me by graduate students and teachers whom

I know. All stories are true. I did not make up any of these vignettes. Many of the stories have been decontextualized to protect the guilty. At times, I have changed names, ages, context, etc., but the central core of the experience has been maintained. Other times, and with permission, I have used the real names of the participants. In this book I have linked theory to practice by providing classroom vignettes that demonstrate what theory might look like in real life.

ORGANIZATION

The organization of this second edition follows the same pattern as the first edition: Critical pedagogy: How in the world did I get into this? What in the world is it? Where in the world did it come from? How in the world do you do it? And why in the world does it matter?

Changes I Have Made in This Edition

The first edition of this book triggered the following two questions more than any others: What is it? How do you do it? I am hoping that this second edition will more thoroughly address these two questions.

The Preface and the Introduction are new. These two new sections will contain stories that capture some of the surprising things I have learned since the publication of the first edition, and because of it. "Welcome to My Real World" has been added in direct response to a pattern of questions that are asked consistently of me when I am invited to speak about critical pedagogy.

Chapter 1 tells the story of students and teachers who taught me that much of critical pedagogy is discovered in that enlightened, and often uncomfortable, space of relearning and unlearning. In this second edition I share new relearning and unlearning experiences. The story of Jonathan, which was in the original introduction, will be updated in this chapter.

Chapter 2 explains how my prior knowledge of Vygotsky became a tool for my understanding of the language and thoughts of critical pedagogy. Eventually, I was able to generate meaning from the perspective of real students and teachers in real classrooms and communities. Definitions have been added and cognitive coathooks are used to connect the parts to the whole.

Chapter 3 traces the roots of critical pedagogy through Latin America, Europe, and North America. This history is enriched with new personal anecdotes from some of the leaders who have touched my life. Their theoretical legacy is portrayed as it turns into practice with classroom and community vignettes.

Chapter 4 has significant revisions. It begins with activities that are new to this edition. In the latter half of this chapter, I will revisit some of the methods that were included previously; however, they have been greatly condensed.

Chapter 5 offers a glimpse of some of my own emerging answers and offers the readers the opportunity to discover critical pedagogy in the context of their own lives.

I have added more Chapter Notes with the hope that readers of this introduction to critical pedagogy will more easily be able to access other books with other perspectives on critical pedagogy. I have updated the bibliography with works I have discovered and rediscovered. These new references have affected my thinking since the publication of the first edition. To all of the authors I am indebted. As I sit surrounded by my treasured books, I often feel fortunate to be enriched by an ever-growing community of scholars who happen to be stacked on my desk and lying in a circle around my computer chair.

A Word About Definitions

"I love the way you don't give us definitions," the teacher said to me, "and I hate the way you don't give us definitions." This captures what so many of you have written and said to me about the first edition. My goal continues to be that readers will make meaning of critical pedagogy based on their own reflections and experiences. However, more definitions are within context, and the Chapter Notes will lead to other definitions and glossaries.

A Word About Language

Edelsky (1996) notes that traditionally we have been taught to keep our academic discourse cool, mitigated, and detached. We come from a tradition of thought that teaches us that advocacy and passion are irrational; detachment equals rationality. Passionate language conjures up unruliness and disorder (Peller, 1987). Passion combined with an oppositional position evokes fears of dethroning, of revolution. However, as noted by Edelsky (p. xxi), it is really style they find objectionable.

I am personally indebted to the esoteric and abstract language of critical theorists. Indeed, it was the very rigor of the language that enabled me to break through several self-imposed intellectual and emotional barriers, which will be mentioned in more detail in the Introduction. However, I am deeply aware that it was only during a very privileged time of my life that I was able to sit alone in a university library month after month and struggle with the ideas of critical pedagogy. I am also mindful of the fact that most of the teachers and students I admire so much will never have this incredible opportunity. Therefore, I choose to break with the academic norms; I choose to deconstruct the deconstructionist language so that students and teachers with incredibly challenging and complex lives and responsibilities will have access to critical pedagogy. I know that readers will bring the context of their own experiences and will construct their own meaning. My greatest wish is that the readers of this book will eventually toss it and move on to Jim Cummins, Paulo Freire, Henry Giroux, Steve Krashen, Peter McLaren, and Tove Skutnabb-Kangas, to whom I am so deeply indebted.

A Word About Pronouns

Most of my life, I always read he/him when referring to an indefinite pronoun. Of course, I knew it meant me. Then I entered a time when I read he/him, and I delicately suggested that it didn't seem to include me. Of course, it includes me I was told. Another phase of my reading began, and I read he/she and him/her. Of course, it meant me and you, but it was so awkward. Now, I am entering another pronoun phase of my life. My options are (a) he/him; or (b) he/she and him/her; or (c) one chapter in he/him and another chapter in she/her. That, too, feels uncomfortable. Therefore, I have decided to do what feels right. The indefinite pronouns I have chosen for this edition are she/her. For me, it is a game of catch-up. Maybe in my lifetime, we'll find the perfect pronoun, but until that day comes, of course, I mean everyone.

Changes I Have Not Made

At the end of the first edition, I asked the readers to write their own world. And write they did. In the margins; in the little boxes; in e-mail and in letters to me. Thank you. None of us writes alone, and the readers of the first edition are writing the second with me. Even the horseshoe person and fertilizer person are writing this book with me. I thank all who have shared their thoughts about my thoughts.

No one has received more input on this book than I. I am well aware of what readers love and what readers don't love. I even have a pretty good understanding of who likes (and who doesn't like) which pages. And I know which pages are never mentioned. Here is my rule-of-thumb for writing the revision: if the pages sang to many readers, I left them in— even if it were a new song for some readers. If the pages did not sing, I cut them out.

The first edition provided me with many surprises that are the continuing story of my learning-relearning-unlearning. In this second edition, my plan is to share some of these surprises.

Changes the World Has Made

We are in a more difficult sociocultural political climate than when the first edition was written. Public education is under greater threat than before. Simple answers to complex questions are more appealing to more people. Critical perspectives are more criticized. Although this book is not about oppressive forces that I fear are gaining momentum, I will reference several, particularly when speaking about unlearning.

ACKNOWLEDGMENTS

It is often said that writing is a solitary process. Not so. Many have helped me write this book by sharing their thoughts with me. I can never repay your generosity of ideas and spirit; I can only pass it on.

To the graduate and credential students in California, Arizona, and Mallorca, thank you for the professional and personal interactions which enrich my life.

To my friends and colleagues at CSU Stanislaus, thank you. I am glad I am with you as we move forward together. As this book was written from South Dakota while my materials were in California, several of you searched shelves, piles of papers, boxes of books, and collections of journals in order to fax, email, or snailmail me the exact citation at the perfect moment. Thank you Sheri, Jeannie, Janet, Chris, Brenda, Fay, Meg, and Fernando. Even my friends at the local county office of education came to my rescue with the right source when I needed it. Thank you Claudia, Beti, and Olivia.

To my friends in Arizona, thank you for taking good care of me and my dear desert. Pam Sharpe, Nick Lund, Nancy Blitz, and Natalie Hess, thank you for providing opportunities to pursue pedagogy together. Carole Edelskey, thank you for sharing your ideas during the preparation of this edition.

To my friends on the Internet, Ken and Yetta Goodman, Jill Mora, Jim Crawford, Maragret Moustafa, Pat Eastman, Yiqiang Wu, and LeAnn Putney, your generous communications have enriched my pedagogy. Alastair Pennycook, thank you for thinking about my thoughts about your thoughts.

To Dan Bratten who took an aesthetically-challenged text-only copy of this book and turned it into an aesthetically-pleasing document in several long days, I thank you from the bottom of my harddrive and my heart.

Critical pedagogy asks us to unlearn *tolerance* of the "other." Critical pedagogy asks us to move forward from tolerance; it calls us *to accept, to respect,* and even *to celebrate* the "other." Think about it, how would you feel if I said that I can *tolerate* you? The "other" is not just about diversity of race, class, culture, and gender; it is also about diversity of thought. To my editor, Art Pomponio, thank you for this diversity of thought. In many ways we are *each other's other:* You are urban, I am rural; you are east; I am west; you are rational; I am passionate; you are attracted to gourmet cooking; I am interested in plain eating. My study of critical pedagogy has taught me that my perspective is just that: mine. Others' perspectives are inherent within the theory of critical pedagogy. Art, you and I turned this theory into practice. Thank you for critically reading and responding as we negotiated the "other" and created ideas which broaden the perspective of each of us and, hopefully, expand the discussion of critical pedagogy from *tolerance* to *celebration* of the "other."

To Addison Wesley Longman's reviewers, who took time to read and respond quickly and critically, I am indebted. Your multiple perspectives raised questions I had not considered, and I have used your thinking to inform mine. Thank you to: Robert Sherman, University of Florida; and Kim Moore, UC-Riverside.

It so often seems that the right person moved into my life at the right time. This could be said of many of the previously mentioned friends. At other times, significant people came into my life early and stayed for the long trip. Steve Krashen, Jim Cummins, and Tove Skutnabb-Kangas, thank you for staying. My thoughts grew from yours.

To Sharon and your very able helpers Jan, June, and Grandma, you have searched and found everything from important scraps of paper to cherished books in second-hand book stores. Thank you for this and your enduring friendship. Grandma, the quilt you made for me keeps my legs, my feet, and my soul warm as I write.

To my ever-growing family: Dean, Dawn, Bo, Lisa, Michael, Wyatt, and Luke. Thank you for our shared life of learning, laughter, and love. Dawn, thank you for critically reading every vulnerable, fragile new paragraph. You not only read, but you are written in every page of this book. As you flit through the house talking honestly about meaningful things, I am empowered and ennobled to reach to your level of expectations of authenticity and honesty. For example, I wrote the new preface and introduction for this second edition during Thanksgiving on the ranch. Twenty minutes is probably the longest time period I wrote without being interrupted. If I were not encircled by this love, I could not write honestly of my own experiences.

Whether you are with me at my home on the range or my home on the Internet, I hope you find your contributions on these pages.

Joan Wink

Introduction
Welcome to My Real World

Pedagogy is to good interactive teaching and learning in the classroom as critical pedagogy is to good interactive teaching and learning in the classroom and in the real world (see Note 1).

The publication of the first edition of this book enriched my life with new ideas, new friends, and a couple of surprises. The first surprise has been a group of questions that I am continually asked: What is it like to write a book? Where do you write? When do you write? What are publishers and editors like? What do they do? What do you do? This group of questions makes me relearn the importance of context, which we will talk more about in the section on Vygotsky in chapter 2. This group of questions also makes me realize that many people want to write. Because of these continuing questions, I have chosen to begin this second edition with a peek into the context of my life as it relates to writing and thinking.

The first edition of this book was written in the midst of my real life. I was teaching full-time, and most pages were written between 3 a.m. and 6 a.m. and on weekends. I longingly watched other professors go away and write in peace during their sabbaticals.

The day I received my first copy of my first book was an important one in my life. That readers later asked so many questions about where I was and what I was doing at the moment amazes me. The truth is that I couldn't wait to get my hands on a copy of my own book.

"You sure do clean up well," the UPS man said to me that hot August day standing on the prairies when he realized that the package I had just

1

opened contained a book with my picture on the back. He was used to delivering packages of books to me, but a book I had written was a new experience for him, and certainly for me.

"Can I take this copy home, just for tonight?" he asked. "I'll return it tomorrow," he promised, even though I knew that he lived 100 miles away. He eagerly took the book from me and started to leaf through the new, clean pages. You can imagine a UPS truck with the side panel doors wide open in August on the hot, windy prairies: Dust and dirt were flying in all directions, outside the truck and inside the truck. In fact, much of this prairie dust had come to rest on the driver's hands, which were now rapidly examining my first copy of my first book.

This is not how I thought it would be for the initial perusal of my first book. I can still see the handprints on those virgin pages, and I can still feel the absolute joy we were both experiencing as our eyes (and his hands) devoured the pages. There we were, shoulder to shoulder, heads bent, standing on the prairies, laughing and debating who would keep the book that night. He reasoned that I had written the book, so I didn't need to read it. I reasoned that I wrote the book; I want the book. Those fingerprints are still on those now well-worn pages and remind me that things never quite turn out the way I imagined. Life is often filled with contradictions, ironies, and unforeseen joys.

My life in schools (McLaren, 1998) has been much the same (see Note 2). When I started teaching, I imagined that it would be predictable, controllable, and safe. I will teach, I thought; and they will learn. Like Edelsky (1996), I was sure that I would be cool, mitigated, and detached; I was confident that every moment would be rational. My experiences in schools have taught me something different. Human relationships are at the heart of schooling (Cummins, 1996, p. 1). Indeed, it has been the passion and the personal interactions that have put the power in pedagogy for me. Although many of my experiences in schools are not as I thought they would be, it is only the study of critical pedagogy that made me realize that the potential of pedagogy is all about people. I thought my life in schools would be about me, teaching. I now think that Paulo Freire was right: Education is radically about love (N. Millich, personal communication, November 3, 1998; see Note 3).

Now I am no longer longing for a sabbatical; I am experiencing one as I write this second edition. Again I am having to unlearn some of my previously long-held assumptions, this time about peaceful sabbaticals. Once again I am reflecting on the amazing surprises, and even contradictions, in life and learning.

I am revising the first edition from my little writing nook on the second floor of our 1910 ranch house on the prairies during the winter of 1998–1999. My grandmother moved from a sod hut into this house in 1910;

it must have been a castle to her. It is not a castle but comfortable, peaceful, and spiritual. The only source of heat is an oil furnace in the dirt basement; the hot air is vented through one large grate on the floor of the living room of the first floor. The grate is at the bottom of the stairs to the second floor, and my writing nook is at the top of the stairs on the north wall. I have a little electric space heater to keep my feet warm, and I write with a home-made woolen quilt wrapped around me. I often look out my north window to a dark and even threatening sky. The sun is now setting in the west at about 4:03 p.m., and we still have one month and 3 days before the winter solstice. The dark evenings are long, and I write whenever I can find time: mornings, afternoons, or nights. My goal is to be writing the last sentence as I watch the northern lights.

I always find it humbling to write about Paulo Freire. And sometimes, my real world is also humbling. Yesterday I was so engrossed in updating the section on Paulo Freire that I failed to notice that from my window, which faces north, a truck was coming down the lane. Suddenly, I heard a loud banging on the outside door. I did a quick save on my computer, ran down the stairs, and went to the door. There was a stranger, a truck driver, who had a delivery for my husband. I quickly explained where he could find him and hurriedly said a good-bye as I wanted to get back to Freire. As I was closing the door and the man was walking away, he turned back and yelled to me, "You want to be sure to take dinner (the noon meal) to the field for your husband. I know he will be working hard."

I returned to my writing about Paulo Freire, and the phone rang. It was another person I had never met. Here is our conversation:

> *"Hello," I answered.*
> *"Uh, hello," he replied. "Is this the missus?"*
> *"Yes," I said.*
> *"Is your husband there?" he continued.*
> *"No," I answered.*
> *"Well, I need you to go out to the fertilizer tank and find the serial number. It is on the tongue between the hitch and the jackstand. I'll just wait here on the phone," he clarified for me.*

These ironic interruptions are reflective of my real world, which followed me to sabbatical. I am aware that most of my colleagues envision that I write in the pure peace of the prairies. Only someone who has lived here would understand when Norris (1993) speaks of the "silencing of the prairies."

In the first edition two concepts triggered the greatest reaction. First was the page I wrote on silencing. It is one of those pages that I know some will love and some will not. I have left it in this second edition. I can predict that the reactions will follow gender lines, although silencing takes place in a far broader arena: along lines of race, class, culture, ethnicity, and even geography, as explained by Norris (1993). When we get to the part that caused the second greatest reaction, I will also alert you to it.

Did I stop writing and take "dinner" to the field? No. Did I stop writing and go out to check the serial number on the fertilizer tank? No. Most of my life I would have, and I would have smiled while doing it. Now I say no, and I smile at the amazing contradictions in my real world. I know you have them, too. The links between life and learning in schools become more and more apparent to me the longer I live. I believe that critical pedagogy has helped me see this.

Recently, I kept a running list of interruptions for three days. The list grew faster than my book, so I quit. On the yellow stickies of my computer, I made the following notes about other activities that went on while I wrote:

- Looking out my north window I have seen deer, antelope, fox, coyotes, eagles, hawks, wild canaries, and skunks. I had to stop the dogs from chasing the skunks.

- We are remodeling the house and adding a screened-in porch; the carpenter does a lot of pounding, and he loves to talk to me about his artwork. In fact, he is an exquisite artist. If I were to describe for you his jewelry, carved from deer antlers, inlaid with various colors made from crushed rock, and outlined with ashes from a Lakota Sioux religious ceremony, you would all stop reading and try to find him to buy his jewelry. So I won't do that.

- The fax machine is beside my computer. In the past three days I received faxes on growing echinacea; faxes from professional organizations; faxes for political activities; faxes for fantasy football; and faxes about bulls for sale. This stack of faxes makes me think that there is a lot of diversity in my real world.

- One of my grandsons is sitting behind my computer chair. He has just discovered a box that contains mounds of colored paper that had gone through a paper shredder. His delight is infectious. I muse on what is more important: playing with the paper with him or writing a paragraph.

- I have cooked and served nine meals and taken many coffee breaks in these three days. I used to think that I had to serve homemade cookies during coffee breaks. Now, in my more liberated phase of life, I serve M&Ms—the multicolored ones with almonds in the middle. I notice that people really do eat the blue ones first. As I cook and serve, I relearn what Hasselstrom (1987) means: "In these days of working couples, I wonder if only farm wives still regularly cook three meals every day. It seems to me I just get well immersed in a story or a poem when it's time to cook again" (p. 80).

- I have stopped to clean mud and manure from the porch, the kitchen floor, the living rug, the recliner chair, the bathroom—I am suddenly realizing that it apparently does not make it to the second floor bedrooms. It pleases me immensely to know that there is none up here where I write.

- I have washed, dried, folded, and put away seven loads of clothes. Water is so valuable on the prairies that I try never to wash unless I have a full load. The water is hard, and the whites yellow; the colors fade.

- I stopped only once to help move cattle. It took six hours and was pure joy. Buttercup is the name of my horse. In chapter 5, I will tell you much more about Buttercup and power and fear of power.

- I went for four walks with my dogs on the prairies. I am constantly amazed at the diversity of grasses. This makes me think:

  Prairies: the greater the diversity, the healthier the environment.

  Perspectives: the greater the diversity, the broader the thought.

  People: the greater the diversity, the better the democracy.

- I had to explain to two men how to get to the field to change a flat tire on the tractor. The thought of changing a flat on a tractor made my real world seem simple.

- I have had innumerable conversations with my husband about preparing the fields and prairies for next year. This always makes me reflect on how much we as educators are like farmers and ranchers. We prepare the soil; we plant seeds; we fertilize; we cultivate; we plow; we pray for a favorable season from outside elements. Critical pedagogy is very similar, and it makes us look more critically at ourselves and the role we are playing in the production (or reproduction) process. Critical pedagogy makes us see more clearly the effects of the environment. Critical pedagogy also gives us the courage to plow and the patience to wait.

I marvel at the outside influences on my life. I also marvel at the outside influences on teaching and learning. Critical pedagogy enables us to see those influences more clearly and to articulate them. Critical pedagogy also enables us to take action in our real world when necessary.

Now here is the point: Each of us has her own real world. It informs us; it enlightens us; it amuses us; it challenges us. And, each of our worlds is a part of who we are. Each of our worlds contributes and enriches us and others. Our own unique real world is the culture we know best; it is where we feel most at home; we speak the language; we know the perspective. No one's real world is the best; it is just what we know. No one's culture is the best; it is just what we know. No one's language is the best; it is just what we know. Critical pedagogy has enabled me to appreciate and celebrate others' ways of knowing—even when I don't understand and may not have experienced them.

First, I share my real world because you asked. Second, I share my real world for all readers who are future writers. You have a book inside you waiting to be written. You know it; I know it. You may believe that authors live and write in a world you will never know. Authors are people writing in their own world. Our real worlds are unique, busy, and often exhausting.

It is the legacy of my real world that informs my perspective. It is the legacy of critical pedagogy that gives me the courage to express my perspective. I am confident that critical pedagogy will encourage you to read and write your world.

Not only was I surprised that so many readers wrote to ask me questions about reading and writing in my world, but I was also surprised at the diverse reactions along gender lines. The irony is that one of my greatest fears with the publication of the first edition was that my feminist colleagues would believe that I had not been strong enough on our shared interests. Instead, the exact opposite has happened. My formal educational experiences have been in the world of multicultural and multilingual education; however, I am limited in feminist pedagogical academic study. A reader of the first edition once wrote to me: "It feels like you are reading us, while we are reading you." However, when it came to gender issues, many readers were reading me critically. I was writing the word, and the readers were reading the world (see Note 4). Often in the first edition, I thought I was writing about dominant and dominated cultural groups, and readers were reading men and women.

Some of What Was Not Said in the First Edition

In what follows are two examples of what was not said in the first edition but apparently came out between the lines.

First, a long time ago, when I was about 30 years old and lived in an evil state far, far away, I completed my units for a master's degree, wrote my thesis, and went to turn it in to my lead professor. He told me that I would receive his signature on my completed degree plan if I would sleep with him.

I walked out the door and never looked back. I, like many graduate students and teachers, had a very demanding and complex life: a 3-year-old, a 6-year-old, a husband changing jobs, and a U-Haul truck sitting in front of the house. I never mentioned it again, not to my family, not to anyone. This time period still remains blank on my resume. For years I worried that others would find out about my failure. My adult children will learn about it when they read this.

I Dropped Out

Mostly, I recall the shame I felt. It is now clear to me what was taken from me that day: Time, money, a master's degree, courage, self-confidence are a few of the things that come to mind. Critical pedagogy has also enabled me to understand more fully the role I was playing in that process. I never should have walked away; I should have taken action to make sure that he walked away from that university and carried the shame, not me. Critical pedagogy calls us to action.

Here is what happened the next few years: I stayed away from universities for fear that I would be found out. Eventually, I worked toward a second MA degree in another state; I remember worrying that this university would wonder about those empty years on my resume. When I successfully completed that MA, I was sure it was just luck. So, I did yet another MA, apparently to assure myself that I could. So let me count, I now have three MAs: two for which I received diplomas and one that was left in that evil state far, far away. I was 44 years old when I started working toward my Ph.D. and began exploring critical pedagogy. The language was new to me but not the ideas. In 1991, I was finally ready to begin my first tenure-track assistant professor position.

Coincidentally and simultaneously, the fall of 1991 was the time of the Anita Hill/Clarence Thomas hearings. I, like many, sat on the couch and watched. I was spellbound. After a few days of this, I said to my husband, "No one ever made a pass at me in the professional world. Listen to all these stories. You would think this was rampant in the workplace." I stayed on the couch, turned back to the television, and suddenly burst into tears. It all came back. I may have conveniently arranged to forget it, but apparently I was still carrying it. The memories consumed me and shocked me. Shocked my husband, too.

When Wolf (1993) writes about the Anita Hill/Clarence Thomas hearings as a time of genderquake in the United States, I now recognize that the earth shook for me, too.

)

We may never know the truth or falsehood of what was alleged in the hearing room, but what is certain is that something critical to the sustenance of patriarchy died in the confrontation, and something new was born. The sight of a phalanx of white men . . . showing at best blank incomprehension, and at worst a cavalier, humiliating disregard for women's reality and testimony, was a revelation to the nation's women of the barrenness of democracy without female representation, as well as being an unmasking of male authority. (p. 5)

Second, it was not long after this when I learned over a cup of coffee with a male colleague that my men friends, with comparable professional experience, were paid more than I at the university. I remember him saying: "Joan, I could never be you; I couldn't afford to support my family." For a brief second, I remember thinking that the issues of power that revolve around gender were not mine; I was more at home in the world of power as it relates to cultures and languages. The legacy of critical pedagogy flashed in front of me: to name; to reflect critically; to act. This time I did not walk away, and the yellow roses planted in my front yard are my personal and, up until now, private celebration of the three-year battle it took for me to convince a large educational system that social justice does matter. Nieto (1996) says that critical pedagogy is an exploder of myths. It sure exploded a few for me.

Critical pedagogy has made me look back and rethink my life in schools. Maybe it wasn't as I first thought. Critical pedagogy helped me to unlearn, to unpack, and to rewrite my experiences. Critical pedagogy is about reading and writing our real world. Critical pedagogy gives us the courage to say what we have lived.

Remember, I told you that there were two places that caused the most reaction in the first edition? The first was the page on silencing. I have added to it. The second was the page of the A Team and the B Team. I have added to it as well, based on some of my B Team experiences in life. I was not able to write about this in the first edition, but now I am. I thank the readers who read between the lines for their support in my continued re-learning and unlearning.

People consistently tell me that my book is personal. Yes, I know. I am writing about what I have personally experienced in life and learning. Critical pedagogy has enabled me to name, to reflect critically, and to act. Nieto (1996) says that this three-step process need not be linear and direct. That was true for me. It took a couple of kids, a couple of grandkids, one husband, more than a couple of decades, and several states. Linear or not, I hope that critical pedagogy will be as powerful in your life.

This is a personal and passionate book about my critical reflections on pedagogy, the interaction between teaching and learning.

PROLOGUE

The Story of Jonathan

I learned to read by way of phonics in the first grade. First, I learned the individual letters and their sounds; from letters and sounds, I moved to individual words; from words, to sentences, to paragraphs, to pages, to stories. I learned to read by building up the parts; bottom to top. Reading specialists would say I was a parts-to-whole reader. Some would say that phonics gets the credit. I slowly and carefully put the puzzle together piece by piece. In school I read every assignment, every chapter, every set of comprehension questions at the end of chapters, every spelling list, every grammar assignment. I read everything I was told to read; I got good grades and graduated at the top of my high school class. One problem: I hated to read. I read only the exact number of pages assigned; I never took a book home to read for pleasure. I went to college and continued the same pattern. I spent every free moment in the library, got good grades, graduated with honors in literature, and yet I still hated to read.

When my children were babies, I started to read to them. The baby books said I should, so I did. With our first child, Dawn, something started to change: I loved the big black-and-white checkered book, *The Real Mother Goose*. I thought *Winnie the Pooh* had been written just for me. By the time we got to *Charlotte's Web*, I was hooked on books. I used to secretly read *The Secret Garden* even when Dawn was asleep. With our son, Bo, I broadened my literary base. I probably have read *The Three Little Pigs* several thousand times, and I still huff and puff with vigor. *Pecos Bill* was the highlight of Bo's preschool years at home. From there he moved on to BMX magazines, and we both became authorities on racing bikes. After BMX magazines, he moved on to motorcycle books. From there, he jumped right into Stephen King and left me far in the dust. It was at this point in my life that I had to find my own books to read. I was probably about 30 years old.

When did Dawn and Bo learn to read? I have no idea, but it was before kindergarten. One day Dawn came home from kindergarten crying because the librarian wouldn't let her check out *The Secret Garden*. The librarian said it was too hard for kindergartners and only third-graders could have it.

The same librarian would only let the students check out one book at a time, a rule that Dawn hated. One day she checked out her one allotted book, shoved three more inside her T-shirt, and headed for the exit. She had detention for a week. (This meant that we all had detention for a week, as we lived in the country an hour away from school.)

Dawn and Bo learned to read the opposite from me. Reading specialists would say that they were whole-to-part readers. They looked at the picture of the whole puzzle first and then put the pieces together. Do they love to read? Yes. Do they read for pleasure? Yes.

When I first started to notice all of this, it seemed like a contradiction. How could my kids possibly learn to read if they didn't do the same thing I had done? Didn't I need to teach them the sounds, the letters, the words first? However, it was clear to me that they were not interested in the *parts*. They wanted the *whole* story again and again and again. Since that time, I have been very interested in the various ways that children learn to read and read to learn. This is what triggered my interest in holistic and critical teaching and learning. It seems that many kids who were read to as little children learn to read and love to read. Homes with books and ideas and love seem to produce kids who love to read—except for Jonathan, who is a 12-year-old contradiction in my educational space. From Jonathan I had to unlearn much of what I thought to be true. Jonathan taught me that one-size-does-not-fit-all when it comes to reading and teaching and learning.

Jonathan comes from an enriched family. He has food, love, and lots of laughs. His dad is a lung specialist; his mother is the best-read person I know; and his brothers and sister are great kids. Now that I am at a point in my life where I philosophically understand why kids with books learn to read, I must still be alert to the exceptions. I listen to the whispering of the juxtaposition.

Jonathan spent two years of preschool in a two-way Spanish-English immersion where 50 percent of the students were English speakers, and 50 percent of the students were Spanish speakers. His two oral languages grew rapidly. Jonathan flourished as he ran and played in this bilingual context. When he spoke to the English role model teacher, he used only English. When he needed something from the Spanish role model teacher, he switched to Spanish without hesitation. In class and on the playground, he used either language with his peers.

Jonathan entered kindergarten and was able to continue in a two-way immersion program. This program had been well established years ago. The first group of students had already graduated from high school and were now bilingual college students. Some of these students were European

Americans, some were Mexican American, but all were biliterate and continuing to achieve academically.

In this program Jonathan had the best of everything: the best teachers, pedagogy, field trips, fish bowls, crayons, and curriculum. Jonathan's prior experiences and this school setting could not have been better. We were ready for Jonathan's emergent literacy to begin.

He didn't read in kindergarten; we waited. He didn't read in first grade; we waited and started to worry. He didn't read in second, nor third, nor fourth, nor fifth grade. I called reading specialists in several states. I read every book on reading I could find. The message consistently was read to him, talk with him about ideas, love him, give him success in other areas. We did it all. Jonathan's applesauce won a blue ribbon at the state fair. He became an avid photographer and joined a senior citizen's photography club where every member adored him. In his neighbor's garage he developed an interest in and ability in carpentry. Still he couldn't read. We worried more and tried everything: stories, phonics, print-rich environment, dittos, sandpaper letters, Cool Whip words, more stories, more love. With each passing year, we became less philosophically grounded and more eclectic. We tried everything I believed in and everything I didn't believe in, and I don't like to admit this to you.

Jonathan's two oral languages and knowledge continued to grow at a rapid rate. He knew so much, but he couldn't write about it, nor could he read.

Tests. Tests. And, more tests. Jonathan knew every specialist in the district. Jonathan soon began to feel very bad; his self-esteem suffered. His family, his neighbors, and his teachers continued to focus on what Jon could do and not what he couldn't, but we were all in agony. The special services division of the district assessed Jonathan with *every* test available. Jon and his parents suffered through interminable student-study-team meetings, where each time new well-meaning strangers offered new advice based on yet another test.

Finally, in the summer of his fifth grade, his desperate parents enrolled Jonathan in a private program that focused on auditory discrimination deficit, a problem that several tests had ruled out long ago. The teacher of this program said it would be different. It was. It was prohibitively expensive; the students had to focus for four hours at one sitting; Jon would have to go every day; the parents had to commit to a minimum of 40 hours.

I was the least optimistic of all. This program was everything that I knew wouldn't work. This was a wreck waiting to happen. I understand why Jonathan's parents were willing to try, but I was confident that this would only do more harm to Jonathan's failing self-concept. He did not need another failure.

After his initial visits, Jonathan called me long distance and excitedly asked me to come and watch him read. I jumped in the car and drove several hours and arrived in time to attend the next session with him. We entered the living room, which had been transformed into a type of reading laboratory for Jon with pictures of tongues and mouths in various positions, manipulatives, cards, and a board that reminded me of a three-dimensional Monopoly game. Jonathan sat down and focused on the instructions and the sounds he was to make. He knew where his tongue went for every sound. He proudly explained the difference in sounds and talked excitedly about "lip poppers" and "lip tappers." He knew the difference between "fat" sounds and "skinny" sounds; he didn't confuse the "coolers" and the "tongue coolers." By breaking down words into very, very small parts, Jonathan was able to break through the decoding barrier.

"Now, I am finally starting to read, Joan," he proudly told me. For years I have studied the debate regarding whether we learn to read from whole-to-part or from part-to-whole. Does it help us to have a picture of the puzzle before we start to put the puzzle together? Yes. Does it help us to know the story before we begin to read each page, each paragraph, each sentence, each word, each sound? Yes. If families love reading and spend wonderful times reading to their children, will the children begin to read and love to read? Yes. Except for Jon.

In the first edition, Jonathan was reading and writing in the sixth grade. He struggled with spelling tests. I remember when he tried to memorize the word, *aboard*. Jonathan did not know this word, had never used this word, and could see no need for it in his life. He said to his mom, "Even if I learn to spell it by Friday, I still won't know it next Monday."

"Let's move on to social studies," his mom replied, recognizing that he understood far more than how to spell *aboard*. The two of them began to talk about the various people who live in the world, as part of the social studies assignment. Suddenly, Jonathan became very excited and said to his mom, "*People. People.* Now there is a word I could really use. I'll learn how to spell *people*, and I'll always know it." He knew it on Friday, and he knew it the following Monday, and he still knows how to spell it.

Jonathan is the whispering of the juxtaposition for me. He is the voice of the *other*. Jonathan teaches me to keep learning from the opposites of my beliefs. After writing this story, I sent a copy to Jonathan and his mom. Jon was delighted to read about himself but disappointed with me.

"Mom, she didn't get it," he groaned.
"What didn't she get?" his mom asked.

*"She missed the whole point. The reason I'll always remember
how to spell* people *is because I need to know it."*
No, Jonathan, I didn't miss the point. I get it.

The Journey of Jon Continues

Since the first edition was published, the journey of Jonathan continues. He
is now 15 years old and 6 feet 4 inches. Simply put, Jon is a joy. He is a ter-
rific citizen of his school, church, and community. His literacy development
continues to raise subtle questions, which can often be a prelude to relearning and unlearning for me.

For example, Jon makes me relearn that meaning matters. Jon has begun to write notes to girls. Usually, Jon does not worry about his less-than-
perfect spelling; spell-check works fine for assignments. However, when it
comes to note-writing (one of the most underrated literacy activities of adolescents), Jon wants it perfect. Suddenly, he is self-conscious about his
spelling and asks his mom to check his notes. However, he always gives her
clear and concise instructions: "Don't READ it; just check the spelling."

Jon's family has always had great expectations for him, so when, as a
freshman in high school, he was assigned to read a classic by Charles Dickens, I listened intently. I wondered if *Great Expectations* would be meaningful in his life. Jon's middle name is Dickens, and it seemed that this might in
some mysterious way "empower" him to decode this old English novel. As it
turned out, his mother finally read it aloud to him. I think Jon will remember
the hours spent with his mother as she read, and I think he will remember a
story she told him. Dickens was paid by the word when he sold his stories
in serial form. "That might be the reason why he devotes so much into describing how someone cut and buttered a piece of bread," Jon replied. I am
wondering if you and I have such abiding memories of our high school experiences with Charles Dickens.

At the same time that Dickens was required reading in school, Jon
found a Dennis Rodman book at the local book store, and I received a phone
call from his mom.

*"Joan, Jon wants to buy a Dennis Rodman book, and he has
saved his allowance for it," his mom began.*
"Nancy, you are the mom who ONLY wanted your son to read,"
I responded. "Let him read."

From Dickens to Rodman in the same week initiated more unlearning
about literacy for us. It seemed a safe and far away time when his mother

and I worried about sounds or whole stories. There is no one perfect way to literacy. Families and teachers need to do whatever is necessary to lead kids to books; the power of literacy will open the door to the great diversity of thought. Books will tell Jon about the "other." I have every confidence that Jon will continue to read the word and the world very well.

CONTRADICTIONS AND CHANGE

Now, why in the world am I beginning a book on critical pedagogy with a story about Jonathan's reading? Critical pedagogy is to literacy as theory is to practice; they are inseparable partners in schools. Because I am a holistic teacher and learner, Jon's inability to read at the prescribed time was an affront to my beliefs. It slowly began to dawn on me that Jonathan and I were living what all those critical pedagogy books called the *other*.

What is the *other*? It is all I haven't experienced. It is what I don't know and understand. It is the upside-down to my right-side-up. For each of us, the *other* is unique. My *other* need not be yours. However, many of us are often uncomfortable with the *other*. The antithesis does not affirm. The *other* asks us questions, and our answers don't fit. This text is filled with stories of the *other* and how students and teachers have reacted to it. I wanted you to see how I reacted when it happened to me.

When Jonathan's parents asked me why he wasn't reading, I tried to explain it away based on my own ways of knowing. Later, I became a desperate eclectic, which I hate to acknowledge. Multiple tests for Jon and lots of specialists had eliminated many possible explanations. My years of observation and reflection had simply used up my literacy knowledge base. The well was dry. Eventually, I had to admit to Jonathan's parents and to myself the truth: I just didn't know why.

Finally, Jon's parents found pieces of the answer in the *other*. Does this mean that all my critical and holistic ways of knowing are bad and wrong? I doubt it. Critical pedagogy has taught me that education is rampant with complexities, contradictions, multiple realities, and change. It has taught me that I don't know everything. I love and hate the Jonathan story.

In my preparation to be a teacher, no one ever told me about contradictions in education. No one ever told me about change in education. However, I am learning that contradictions and change are fundamental for critically teaching and learning in the twenty-first century. Lately, I have been thinking a lot about these two important topics and would like to share my musings with you. Reading books about critical pedagogy forced me to see the contradictions and changes in education—even when I didn't want to see them.

Jonathan is a contradiction in my educational space. My observations and reflections of Jon teach me that:

- I must continually challenge my long-held assumptions;
- I must let practice inform my theory;
- I must continually build theory that informs my practice;
- I must find new answers for new questions;
- I must grapple with multiple ways of knowing;
- I must listen, learn, reflect, and act.

From Paulo Freire and others, I have learned that we all have contradictions in our educational spaces. We all are experiencing fundamental change. We even have oppositional voices in our educational spaces. The trick is to learn from the contradictions, from the change, from the opposite. No one ever said that teaching and learning would be like this. You can imagine my surprise.

The most important legacy that I have received from my study of critical pedagogy is that all of us need to reflect critically on our own experiences and those of others. Then, we need to connect these new thoughts to our own life in new ways. We do not come from a tradition in schools that encourages critical reflection. We, in schools, are often so busy *doing* that we fail to take time for *thinking*. Thinking about important ideas needs some nurturing in our classes. It takes time. The outcomes are not so immediately visible. The outcomes are more difficult to quantify initially, and it looks as if we're not doing anything. Many of us would agree that what we are doing is not working very well.

Jonathan has made me rethink some of my assumptions about the inherent nature of change and contradiction in teaching and learning. Critical pedagogy is the impetus that causes me to reflect and read for more understanding of my past and my future.

Many of the contradictions and changes in education cause conflict within each of us. Critical pedagogy has helped me to understand that this is all a natural part of learning. Let's think about it: How can learning possibly be static? It is inherently grounded in change. I find that when I take time to reflect on the many contradictions and changes, I am more comfortable moving through conflicting feelings and complex understandings. I used to resist; I used to deny; I used to be very uncomfortable whenever I entered this awkward, uncomfortable space of not knowing. Now, I understand more fully that the many paradoxes and contradictions of education are not as painful when we can articulate all of the change that is swirling around us. In fact, it can even be fun.

"I hate ambiguity," the grad student said to me and her classmates.

"No, we must welcome ambiguity; we must relish ambiguity; we must frolic and play in ambiguity, because then we know we are moving along the learning curve," I responded. Since that time, the class and I have had a lot of fun laughing about how much we love and hate this space of ambiguity. The class now recognizes every time we enter its slippery surface.

For me, these contradictions have become the whispering of the juxtaposition. In my educational space, when I bump into a contradiction, I try to imagine the juxtaposition that sits quietly on my shoulder and whispers in my ear to listen and to learn.

This story captures much of what is wrong with education. My process of learning to read was joyless, but I learned. Jon's was joyful, but he didn't learn. I learned because of the accepted traditional approach to reading. The status quo worked for me. Jonathan learned only when we entered into the nontraditional approach, which, at least for me, was unacceptable. It was only because his parents had the courage and patience to break with the status quo that Jon learned to read. The good news of this story is that Jonathan and I both continue to learn, and finally, we both love to read, although Jonathan got to that point far earlier in life than I did!

The shimmering differences are what we feel as we continue to walk down our unique learning paths; they cause the dissonance we feel when we are at the crossroads of contradiction. At this enlightened—and often uncomfortable—educational space, relearning and unlearning begins.

LOOKING AHEAD FOR ELUSIVE ANSWERS

I, like you, am constantly searching for those very elusive answers. Of course, what I usually discover is just new questions. My intention is to share some of the milestones along my path as I have searched for answers. I don't believe that my answers need to be your answers, but I am confident that by sharing my searching, something that I say may trigger another thought for you in the context of your life and your learning. Throughout the text, readers are invited to read and write their search for answers with me. The answers we have today are often fleeting because the social, cultural, political, and historical context of our lives will change, and tomorrow will be different.

What questions are most important to you in the context of your life and learning right now?

What are some of your elusive answers?

NOTES

1. For this comment, I am indebted to two Arizona graduate students and teachers, Marta and Consuelo, who shared it during an activity we did in a class. On the chalk board, I had written: Pedagogy is to _____ as critical pedagogy is to _____. The class and I thought their idea captured much about critical pedagogy.

2. I am indebted to the first edition of *Life in Schools: An Introduction to Critical Pedagogy in the Foundations of Education* (1989) by Peter McLaren for opening the door to critical pedagogy for me. It is often said that when one is ready to learn, a teacher will emerge. This book was my teacher. It affirmed what middle and high school students in Arizona had previously taught me. The irony is that McLaren was writing about students in Canada, even though every time I pick up that book, I still see the faces of students from the desert Southwest. My hope is that you are envisioning students who have taught you.

3. Nico Millich, a friend and colleague, and I were brought together by our mutual interest in Paulo Freire and critical pedagogy. He has shared various stories with me of his time in El Salvador with Freire, where he was

when he first heard Freire make this comment. Millich continues to follow his interests through liberation theology.

4. This is a reference to my favorite book by Paulo Freire and Donaldo Macedo: *Literacy: Reading the Word and the World* (1987). I have met many people who say that *Pedagogy of the Oppressed* (1970) by Freire is their favorite. I also encourage you to read the update of *Pedagogy of the Oppressed* which is entitled *Pedagogy of Hope: Reliving Pedagogy of the Oppressed* (1994).

chapter **1**

Critical Pedagogy

How in the World Did I Get into This?

Critical pedagogy has pushed me to reflect on my past and my future. What I have learned from these musings has caused me to see and to know in new ways. The contradictions and the changes have made me stop and rethink what I used to know about teaching and learning.

THE BENSON KIDS: TEACHING IS LEARNING

The truth is that much of what I know about teaching and learning, I learned when I was teaching Spanish and English to junior and high school kids in Benson, Arizona, a rural community in the desert Southwest. Initially, I thought that I will teach, and they will learn. Gradually and painfully, I began to recognize that my assumptions were wrong. In fact, much of the teaching methodology that I had learned previously just didn't seem to work. Much to the students' dismay, I tried it all: grammar-translation, audio-lingual, direct method, notional-functional, silent way, jazz chants, and, our all-time favorite, total *physical* response. I vividly recall the day in class when I decided you could throw erasers only for so long, and then we needed a total *mental* response.

Before I tell you all the secrets these students taught me about teaching and learning, let me introduce them to you. I first met many of these students in 1977 when I started teaching the sixth, seventh, and eighth grades in this small school district.

Within the first 24 hours, they started teaching, and I started learning. I learned all 28 eighth graders' names and faces, only to discover that they had—yes—told me the wrong names. I had other classes but this group was my homeroom class, and I would be spending the majority of my day with them. My new colleagues were quick to warn me about all the "problems" that I had received. The students had many labels, which I have since learned to hate: at-risk, troublemaker, problem child, minority, "limited English proficient," and so on. Many of the families lived in areas that we would today call low socioeconomic communities. It seemed to me that they were just families who were working as hard as they could, and doing the best they could, and trying to enjoy their life a little.

I was hired to teach language arts. You must remember that I came from an English literature and Spanish grammar background. When they asked me if I could teach language arts, I thought, "Sure, *what* could be so difficult? I know about languages and literatures, so I certainly must know about language arts." When I walked into the classroom the first day, I soon learned what could be so difficult. There, lined up on a shelf that ran the length of one wall, were all the texts: 28 light blue spelling books, 28 royal blue basal readers, 28 tan penmanship books, 28 large burgundy grammar books (finally, something I recognized—in fact, I had used it when I was their age), and 28 yellow language arts workbooks. Let's see: 5 × 28 = 140 texts for my eighth graders, and I would have other books for my sixth and seventh graders. I knew I would never be able to keep track of all these books, so my first decision was one of the best I ever made: toss the texts. At that time, I did it out of desperation, but doing so taught me more than several teacher education courses had ever done. The truth is that we didn't really toss the texts; we just left them in nice visible stacks on the shelf in case anyone ever wanted to use them (or see us using them).

On the second day, one of the boys who was considered by his peers to be among the "biggest and baddest" asked a really good question:

> *"If we aren't going to use them books, what are we going to do until June?" Danny, spokesperson of the eighth graders, asked with a hint of challenge in his voice.*
> *"Let's just read and write," I responded.*
> *"Read and write?" they said in unison. "What?"*
> *"Whatever we want," my mouth answered. I can assure you that no one in the room was more surprised than I by my response. But, you must remember that I was just trying to get through the day.*
> *"Anything?" they pushed.*
> *"Anything," I innocently answered.*

That day after school, I drove to Tucson to explore the used book stores. There, on the floor in the back of the store by the gardening books, I found a small, worn paperback entitled *Hooked on Books*, by D. N. Fader and E. B. McNeil, which was published in 1966. I had never heard of Fader, or McNeil, or this book, but it seemed right for the moment. I took the book home and read it cover to cover.

Fader and McNeil had some unusual ideas for the times. They said students should read and then write about their reading in journals. They said teachers should not correct errors but that we should respond meaningfully to what the students wrote. Not correct grammar and spelling errors?! Heresy. Fader also said students could write anything they wanted, and the teacher was only to assign a specific number of pages, which would increase with each passing week. Quantity over quality, I thought. But, remember, I was desperate. I had 28 faces to face the next day, and they were probably expecting me to have some answers.

On the third day with my students, I told them what I had found, and we discussed their ideas. They agreed to go along with me. During this discussion, I also mentioned to the class that I had just read a journal article that said it really didn't matter if I corrected all their errors. The article said they wouldn't learn from my corrections. I vividly recall Albert, who already had a reputation for his behavior, mumbling for me to hear: "I could have told you that." These were disturbing ideas for me because all I could think about was the enormous amount of time I had wasted correcting students' papers with the great red pen.

In those days we had no idea what a journal was so we just used the school-supplied lined paper, which we placed inside the school-supplied construction paper. The first week, I assigned five full pages, both sides, every line filled. The students were shocked and sure they couldn't do it.

My actions in the classroom were now counter to anything I had ever been taught, but I had gone too far to turn back. The students slowly began to find materials to read; even more slowly they began to write. Danny, of course, was the first to issue a challenge. I noticed the magazine, which in those days we called a "girlie" magazine, and knew that every eye in the class was watching. However, my parenting had prepared me for this, and I shot him the ol' "Mom-eye." Today, I would not be so gentle. Today I would grab the magazine and use it for curriculum to demonstrate how little girls and little boys are socialized in different ways in our culture. Danny was lucky; he knew me before I knew about gender biasing.

José was the next to issue a quiet, but direct, challenge. The entire class was busily reading and writing. I was quietly walking among the desks and responding to students. When I came to José, I noticed he was writing rapidly. He had a large book, the Tucson phone book, and he was copying names. Long lists of names filled his blank papers. *Hooked on Books* had prepared me for this. Fader and McNeil told me this would happen. They told me that the student would soon tire of this and would want to move to something that interested him.

"What are you writing, José?" I asked.
"I'm copying the phone book," he replied.
"Where are you in the alphabet?" I asked.
"I'm still on the As," he answered.
"Okay," I said and moved on to the next student.

José never made it to the Bs. From the Tucson phone book, he went right to reading about geography and writing about places he found in the almanac. José eventually graduated with honors in English and in Spanish and is now a pilot in the U.S. military. He has visited most of those places he used to write about.

Each Monday I assigned more pages. Each Friday I went home with a huge stack of messy, dirty, construction-paper journals, each filled with treasures and literacy. The following Monday the students got their journals back with my comments, thoughts, questions, and stickers. I remember the absolute joy and delight I saw on the faces of those "problems" when they read my responses on Monday. I finally quit adding more pages when we hit 30 per week, simply because I couldn't carry everything. I knew Fader and McNeil were on to something powerful when the kids groaned and complained when our free reading and writing time was over.

Remember the blue basals that had been left on the shelf with the other texts? Eventually they were used by one boy, Gilbert, who read every single story in the blue basal. He not only read every story; he thoroughly enjoyed them. Gilbert had been considered a nonreader who had resisted every basal to date. During the spring months, he continued to explore the texts stacked on the shelf and shared his discoveries with me. I think he thought I should have this information. On reflection, I think I was not fooling Gilbert; he knew I needed all the help I could get. I remember in late spring the students took the annual achievement test. As with several other students, Gilbert's reading scores jumped three grade levels.

"What did you do for Gilbert?" the principal asked me.
"What did I do?! What did Gilbert do for himself and for me?" I thought to myself.

The other 27 students and I completely enjoyed the freedom of reading and writing. As the students took control of their own learning, their reading and language scores soared. Gilbert read his texts; the other students read science fiction, history, novels, texts from other classes, and even poetry. I read educational journals. I didn't understand it then, but I do now. From these students, I learned the following:

> Reading improves writing.
>
> Choice Matters.
>
> We get smarter when we write.
>
> We love it when someone responds to our writing.

All my teaching and learning since those years is directly related to my experiences teaching and learning with the Benson kids. We discovered by reading, talking, writing, hearing, experiencing, risking, and musing; we learned together. We learned that it all takes time—the great enemy of public education! Every time I read books about critical pedagogy, I see their faces; I hear their questions; I remember their laughter and tears.

LEARN, RELEARN, AND UNLEARN YOUR WAY TO CRITICAL PEDAGOGY

A group of those students in that 6th grade were in my classes in the 7th, 8th, 9th, 10th, 11th, and 12th grades as their classes and my teaching assignments changed. Teaching and learning with this group of students for six years gave me the courage and patience to learn, to relearn, and to unlearn, which eventually led me to a study of critical pedagogy (see Note 1).

To Learn: Difficult Learning Experiences

The Benson students taught me that we learn by reading, talking, writing, listening, experiencing, doing, engaging, interacting, problem solving, problem posing, and taking risks. And, we do it better if we are in a safe and secure environment with an adult who cares about us. Learners choose what to learn. If it doesn't matter to learners, it doesn't matter.

In my own experience, I can remember several learning experiences that were not wonderful. My doctoral course on statistics, for instance; now, there is something that was not fun to learn. However, there was one great surprise: as promised by his former students, the professor really did eat a piece of chalk in the middle of his lecture on multiple regression. In a class of 50 adult graduate students, I think I was one of 2 or 3 who noticed, but I had been waiting and watching with eager anticipation all semester. If I had to learn stat, at least I was going to get to see the famous prof eat chalk.

Now that I am no longer teaching and learning with the Benson kids, I want you to know who my current students are. I am teaching in a state university. When I speak of my graduate students, I am talking about people who have been up since 6 a.m., washed a load of clothes, got the kids off to school, taught all day, went to an after-school meeting, and arrived at the university for a night class. Yes, I teach tired teachers. Even though my graduate students seem to be very hardy souls, sometimes I can see that learning isn't always wonderful for them, either. For instance, sometimes when students read a new idea or hear a new thought, resistance and denial precede learning. We have all experienced this and probably will again.

To Relearn: Difficult Relearning Experiences

Learning can be very challenging, but the problem is that it always leads to relearning, which is more challenging. I think that relearning often involves a shift in methodology. When I walked into that Benson class, I had to shift my methodology from what I had learned previously to that which I needed to learn from the students. Relearning takes places when kids teach us all those things we didn't learn in teacher education.

Sometimes the students are far enough along the relearning curve to understand that the ideas we generate in class are not for class only; rather, they are to be applied to their own worlds. For example, this is what María wrote:

As I start off each new year in teaching, I have to *relearn* because each class is unique and I can't use the same type of teaching methods or discipline. I never could understand how teachers could come into the first faculty meeting of September and have their lesson plans done for the entire year. Don't we have to base our teaching on the needs of our students?

It's reassuring that in our own struggle with relearning, we are in good company. Paulo Freire criticizes his followers for just being content with his first texts and not reading the critiques he has made of his own work, which show that learning and relearning never end (cited in Gadotti, 1994, p. 88).

To Unlearn: Difficult Unlearning Experiences

Learning and relearning prepare us for unlearning, which is the most challenging. Unlearning involves a shift in philosophy, beliefs, and assumptions. Unlearning is unpacking some old baggage.

When I was a little girl, I learned from my Grandma Grace that the melting pot was a symbol of all that was good. Eventually, I had to unlearn that the melting pot was so wonderful for everyone; some got burned on the bottom. This experience with unlearning was very uncomfortable because it challenged all my previously-held assumptions.

The Sioux Indians, who lived on the reservation two miles away, tried to jump into that pot for the sake of being "good Americans." They tried to talk like Grandma, be like Grandma, think like Grandma, and act like

Grandma, but no matter what they did, they could not *look* like Grandma. By doing what they had been taught was right and good, they gave up their language, their traditions, their beliefs, and, in many cases, their very souls. When they leaped into that hot pot, far too much was boiled away. I finally came to unlearn that the pot is really about power. The melting pot worked for my Grandma, but not for her neighbors.

As a European American feminist from a prestigious West Coast university recently told me:

> *I have long considered myself to be an enlightened feminist. However, my comfortable framework was ripped out from underneath me when I met Pam, an African American feminist, who consistently points out the multiple ways in which the feminist movement is Eurocentric.*

Not only do my friends, colleagues, and experiences lead me to unlearning but also to books (see Note 2).

Unlearning is central to critical pedagogy, even though it often feels terrible. This is good. Does it feel like everything you ever learned, you now need to relearn and unlearn? This is good. At least for me, it often seems that all I ever held to be true about teaching and learning has been called into question. Many of my long-held assumptions have not stood the test of time.

LOOKING AHEAD FOR YOUR STORIES OF RELEARNING AND UNLEARNING

As critical pedagogy forces us to shift from passive to active learning, I invite you to reflect, read, and write with me. What have been some of your most difficult relearning and unlearning experiences?

NOTES

1. Learning-relearning-unlearning: As you will see, others have discovered and assigned different meanings to relearning and unlearning. However, long before I ever heard of Alvin Toffler, relearning and unlearning had

very specific meanings for me based on the context of my own teaching and learning—a good example of generative knowledge. For me, relearning relates to methods. In the 1970s and early 1980s, I was always relearning, relearning, relearning. It seemed that every time I finally knew how to do something in the classroom, I had to relearn it. Relearning can be uncomfortable at first, but eventually, it becomes something we do without thinking. Relearning can be tough, but we know it is doable.

Unlearning for me, however, is something very different. It is fundamentally more painful. It involves a complete reexamination of philosophy, beliefs, and assumptions. It means I have to look seriously at myself and not at others, never a simple task. Unlearning is jumping across the great paradigm. Unlearning took place for me when I moved from behaviorism to transformational teaching and learning. It took decades, and not every moment was wonderful. My most recent experience with unlearning is chaos theory, which once again is teaching me that many of my old assumptions about science are dated, or maybe just wrong. Since the mid–1980s, my teaching and learning has involved a lot of unlearning, which leads to more relearning and back to learning: the great cycle of pedagogy.

Critical pedagogy encourages us to find the magic of personal discovery based on our own lived experiences.

Critical pedagogy encourages each of us to reconstruct the words and thoughts of others so that they become meaningful in our own life! Yes, the pattern of learning-relearning-unlearning can be molded and changed and extended to fit your ways of knowing. Critical pedagogy teaches us not to trust prescriptive recipes. In critical pedagogy we read and reread and we write and rewrite. We take ideas and turn them into action. Please take the process of learning-relearning-unlearning and make it fit your ways of knowing and your experiences.

2. If you want an *unlearning* experience, I encourage you to read Goodman (1998) and Taylor (1998). For any who assume that politics are not a part of education, these two books may challenge some long-held assumptions, and they lead us to learn, to relearn, and to unlearn. It remains to be seen if they lead us to action: That is our job.

chapter 2

Critical Pedagogy
What in the World Is It?

"The whole is greater than the sum of its parts, but it's the parts that make all the difference," the student said to me when we were discussing the language and definitions inherent within critical pedagogy. The first objective of this chapter is to look at some of those parts while always keeping the whole in our vision. For example, it is often said that a definition of *critical pedagogy* is to name; to reflect critically; to act. However, if "to name" is strange and unfamiliar language, a part of the whole is lost. Hopefully, I will make the strange familiar and the familiar strange (McLaren, 1998, p. 167) in this chapter as the parts are integrated with the whole.

Furthermore, even if the parts and whole are integrated, unless the theory and practice are united, we fail to bring critical pedagogy to life. Therefore, a secondary objective of this chapter is to unify the theoretical constructs with classroom practice. A lofty goal indeed: integrating not only the parts with the whole, but also theory with practice. I begin.

DAWN *DOES* CRITICAL PEDAGOGY

"All the toys are old, broken, and dirty," she said as she burst through the door. Dawn had just returned from her first day of teaching bilingual kindergarten in a district that had never had a bilingual program, although the majority of their students historically came from migrant families who spoke Spanish.

"The last teacher left boxes and boxes for my kindergarten students. It's just junk. I snuck out to the garbage and threw it away. There were even teaching materials from the 1950s," she groaned.

Dawn was born in 1968. I know; she is my daughter.

Critical pedagogy teaches us to name, to reflect critically, and to act. In this case, Dawn named it: junk. She critically reflected, probably as she snuck outside to find the garbage. And, she acted: She tossed it. Critical pedagogy helped Dawn to understand that 40-year-old teaching materials in English would not meet the needs of her Spanish-dominant kindergarten students.

DEFINITIONS

One way to begin this chapter would be for me to list several definitions of *critical pedagogy* right now. I am resistant to doing that as readers might be tempted to memorize any one of them as if it were the *one true* definition. Even if you memorize a definition, you'll soon forget it, unless you own it, and it matters to you. As Jonathan taught us, "Even if I know the word *aboard* on Friday, I'll forget it by Monday. But, *people:* Now there is a word I could really use."

"It should be stressed that there is no one critical pedagogy" (McLaren, 1998, p. 227), and therefore, I prefer that we move together through these pages until you create a definition that matters to you. I know. It takes longer this way. It is more difficult this way. But, once you have created some meaning for critical pedagogy for yourself, you will never forget it, and you will be able to enrich your meaning only as you learn and experience more. If you are groaning now, I understand. My grad students understand. They all periodically love and/or hate to learn in this mode of critical pedagogy; it was so much easier when we could just sit passively and repeat what was transmitted. In using this text, you need to engage actively. If you find an idea you love or one you hate or one you don't understand, call a friend and discuss it until you create some meaning.

> They were eager to create a model or framework into which they could slot information. I was intent on letting information do its things. They wanted to get organized at the start; I wanted them to move into confusion. I urged them to create more information than they could possibly handle. I guaranteed them that at some point the information would self-organize in them, crystallizing into interesting forms and ideas. (Wheatley, 1992, p. 150)

Just as I finished writing the previous page, I leaned back in my computer chair and looked around at all of the books on my desk and the floor. It suddenly came to me that several of these books contain marvelous definitions (see Note 1). All of these books have enriched my understandings of the parts and the whole of critical pedagogy. My personal definitions are within the context. It is apparent to me that I still prefer definitions within praxis (integration of theory and practice), rather than in a list in a glossary.

Many people (a.k.a. teachers and students) say they just can't write, but they talk very well. Writing is just talking on paper or a computer monitor. If you have trouble writing, talk with someone or talk with yourself, then capture what you said on a napkin, scrap of paper, or a journal. Or, go to your computer and start "talking at the blank screen" (some call this writing) until you make some sense of your own thoughts. I used to think that I wrote for a grade, or for an assignment, or for someone else. I have finally figured out that I write (a) so someone will respond to my thoughts and/or (b) so I can further develop my thoughts. Critical pedagogy has helped me understand that when I write, I am clarifying my own thinking.

Generative Definitions

Generative literacies and generative knowledges are the focus of much of teaching and learning as we near the end of the century. As an example of each, let us begin with what we will call generative definitions. Define each of the following three words based on your own experiences.

CRITICAL

```



```

Critical is a prodding, probing type of word. It is like the gopher on a computer system that goes in and looks around, then doubles back, and looks again. Our critical perspectives find new ways of seeing and knowing. Within this book, *critical* does not mean bad; it does not mean to criticize. Rather, it means seeing beyond. It means looking within and without and seeing more deeply the complexities of teaching and learning.

PEDAGOGY

```



```

Many years ago I thought that pedagogy was about me, teaching. Now, I think it is far more than that. I think *pedagogy* is the interaction between teaching and learning. Good pedagogies give us that electricity we feel when we are totally focused on the unified process of teaching and learning. Bad pedagogies are, at best, boring and, at worst, painful.

CRITICAL PEDAGOGY

Critical pedagogy is a way of thinking about, negotiating, and transforming the relationship among classroom teaching, the production of knowledge, the institutional structures of the school, and the social and material relations of the wider community, society, and nation state (McLaren, 1998, Summer, p. 45). This definition was added to this second edition in direct response to the many requests I received for a "real" definition. My definitions continue to be woven into the context of theory and practice.

We, as teachers, know that we shouldn't ask students to do something that we don't also do. So, here is one of my definitions of critical pedagogy.

Critical pedagogy is a prism that reflects the complexities of the interactions between teaching and learning. It highlights some of the hidden subtleties that may have escaped our view previously. It enables us to see more widely and more deeply. This prism has a tendency to focus on shades of social, cultural, political, and even economic conditions, and it does all of this under the broad view of history. After looking through the prism of critical pedagogy, it seems clear that the basics aren't as basic as they used to be, or at least not as basic as we used to think.

Now that you have mused and written your definitions, let me share with you some definitions that came from students who have finished their undergraduate work and are just ready to begin a teaching credential program. This was a highly diverse group that had not previously studied critical pedagogy. Together they had discussed and read about the idea for only a couple of days. Their definitions of *critical pedagogy* follow:

- a state of mind, a place of reference;
- a framework from which to build;

- a questioning frame of mind;
- it makes us double-check our action and the action of others;
- it makes me do the best I can;
- it empowers with a perspective needed to ask good questions; it makes me actively commit to do something;
- it makes me see beyond what was taught yesterday.

Now that you know how I feel about definitions, you will appreciate my trepidation in defining *critical pedagogy*. I am fearful to give a definition, but I know very well that my readers want one. In an earlier draft of this document, I attempted to solve this problem by hiding the definitions within paragraphs about teachers and learners. At least I thought I was hiding the definitions.

I was walking through the computer lab and happened to glance down at a paper that a student had beside her computer. I noticed that it was the earlier draft of this document. I slowed my pace and looked more carefully at the hard copy to the side of the computer. I noticed with glee and dismay (oh, those darned contradictions of education) that she had found and highlighted in bright yellow all the definitions of *critical pedagogy* I had placed in various paragraphs.

> *"If I understand this correctly, you don't want to define it for us; rather, you want us to find meaning for it based on our lived experiences," she said.*
>
> *"Yes, that is exactly what I mean," I responded. "But, I noticed that you have found all the definitions I thought I had so cleverly hidden throughout the document. You have highlighted them, even though I thought I had woven them within the context so that each reader would eventually discover and generate her own understandings of this somewhat abstract concept."*
>
> *"Yes, I could tell you didn't want us to memorize your definitions. I could tell you were trying to hide them, but my understanding is that critical pedagogy means we have to look back at our own histories and generate new questions in order to find new answers based on our knowledges, and literacies, and cultures, right?"*
>
> *"Right," I replied.*

Phony, from the True

> *The group was busily solving problems in the third-grade class. The teacher had written on the board:*

Estimation	Actual	Difference

First, the teacher asked the students to estimate how many rocks were in the piles on the table.

"Lots."

"37."

"83."

The children began to guess noisily and happily. When each group decided on their guess, they recorded their numbers on their individual papers and on a chart under the word estimation *on the chalkboard.*

Second, the teacher asked each group to count the actual number of rocks. They began counting each little rock and again recorded their numbers on their papers and on the chart under the word actual. *Many squeals of glee could be heard as the students discovered how many were actually in the pile. The problem of the day was to discover the difference. I noticed that the teacher did not use the word* subtract; *she only talked about finding the difference.*

The students began to talk and think; they soon discovered that talking and thinking were more difficult than guessing and counting. One particular group of four students was noticeably struggling. They debated counting and guessing and adding, while all the time shoving their little pile of rocks around the table. However, no matter what they tried, they could not agree on the difference, nor even how to find it. It seemed that the word difference, *and not the process of subtraction, was the stumbling block. It appeared to me that they knew the concept of subtraction, but the word* difference *stumped them. Eventually, they returned to a discussion of estimation and actual, concepts that they knew that they knew.*

Suddenly, a little African American boy in this group shouted, "I get it! I get it! Let's just take the phony from the true, and we will have it."

His teammates immediately understood and successfully solved the problem through subtraction.

In this particular situation, the students knew the concept, but it was the language that was denying them access to the answer. In order to *subtract,* a concept they already knew, they had to find language that they understood. In addition, when they returned to their discussion of *estimation* and *actual* in order to find the *difference*, they were looking for some previous knowledge to connect with the new knowledge.

The same can be said for the language of critical pedagogy. Sometimes, when we bump into new language, it feels like we are being denied access to the concepts. That is how I felt when I first started reading the language of critical pedagogy. Many teachers and learners have lived the concepts of critical pedagogy, and they know what it is; they just don't know that they know.

Finding the Phony.   We often would like to take the *phony* from the *true*. But, is there ever *one* truth? *One* answer? *One* way of knowing? *One* right way? I doubt it. Certainly not in critical pedagogy. In this chapter, I share the *truth* of critical pedagogy as I have experienced it. I hope that my *truth* is an authentic story that reflects my life in schools. I encourage you to reflect on my experiences, to muse on my musings, to think about my thoughts. However, my intention is *not* to transmit my knowledge as if it were the *one true* knowledge. Together, we will visit and revisit the concepts and language through the filter of real teachers and real students in real classrooms. The theory will be grounded in daily classroom practices so that you, the reader, can discover, generate, create, and internalize your own definitions.

LANGUAGE OF POSSIBILITY—LANGUAGE OF CRITIQUE

It is a common experience for educators initially to become aware of critical pedagogy through the unique language that surrounds it. This language is disquieting; we don't feel at home with new language. When we don't understand language, we are denied access to ideas, to concepts, to thoughts, to people. Where in the world did the language of critical pedagogy come from? Perhaps, the following conversation between twin 6-year-old boys and their mom as they drove in the car will shed some light.

NICOLÁS: Who made up words?
MOM: What do you mean?
NICOLÁS: Who made the words in the whole wide world? Words like *trees* and *bees*?
MOM: How do you think words got made?
NICOLÁS: I don't know.
MICAEL, FROM THE BACK SEAT: White people. White people made them.
NICOLÁS: No, God made them.
MICAEL: White people.
NICOLÁS: God.

[They begin to shout at each other.]

MICAEL: White people.

NICOLÁS: God . . . God was here before people.

MOM: I think people invent words as they need them. (Smith, 1995, p. 250)

It's true, critical pedagogs talk funny, or at least some do, sometimes. Buzz words and jargon. We, in education, are often accused of this. I am personally not attracted to jargon, even though I have been accused of using it. Ouch. I remember a powerful voice (J. Stansell, personal communication, March 20, 1991) saying, "Joan, say what you mean, and mean what you say." It seems that this is my goal in this book. I am fully aware of the dangers I face in fulfilling my goal. In trying to simplify, I cannot slip into simplistic. I want to clarify, not trivialize. I want to expand the language, not reduce it. What do all those words mean? When I started reading about critical pedagogy I felt that others knew, and I didn't. I felt as if I had less value, less status, and less knowledge.

The irony is that this new language helped me break out of previous ways of knowing. Another contradiction! The thing I thought was the barrier (language) was the very thing that helped me break through the barrier. The language of critical pedagogy made me quite crazy at first, and ironically, finally opened the door to more complex understandings for me. The language of impossibility became the language of possibility for me. The gate became the drawbridge. It helped me approach the other, on the others' terms, and not on my presupposed image of the other or what I wanted the other to be. My wish is that when you have finished this book, you will feel at home with the language and ideas of critical pedagogy. Recently, Kitty, a teacher, expressed it this way:

Now that I am studying more and more, I have words that describe my beliefs. Before, I thought they were only mine. Now, I am finding that my beliefs are written about in books.

VYGOTSKY: REACHING BACK TO MOVE FORWARD

In the process of teaching and learning I, like all of you, encountered many new ideas. Sometimes these ideas fit with what we have long intuitively felt but never had the language or courage to express. I struggled to consume this new knowledge. As with Jonathan, I tried everything I philosophically believed in and didn't believe in. The more I learned, and the more I read, the more questions I had. It was a constant process that challenged all of my previously-held assumptions of unlearning.

Finally, in desperation, I decided to try what I had always taught my students: Hook it onto prior knowledge. Construct meaning based on your own knowledge and experiences. My internal dialogue went something like this:

> *"What do I know?" I asked myself.*
> *"Well, I know a little about language. Okay, that is a good starting point. Now, what language person, in particular, might be helpful?" I mused.*
> *"Oh, yes, my old friend, Vygotsky." I answered myself.*

I sat down with my worn and tattered *Thought and Language* (1962). I started to read and reread. I tried to connect thought with language, ideas with words. Vygotsky taught me again that if I had one little thought and one word, I could begin to generate meaning between the two. The words would multiply, and the thoughts would grow. The dynamic relationship between the two would continue to create new meanings.

This is exactly what I did in the early stages of my studying critical pedagogy. First, I grabbed any word of critical pedagogy, just one word. "Anyone can learn one word," I told myself. As the words grew, so did the thoughts, just as Vygotsky said they would (Wink, Putney, & Bravo-Lawrence, 1994, September/October).

In this case, language was the tool to help me understand, but it did not feel as if I were using a tool; rather, it felt as if I were using a process that enabled me to think more deeply and critically. A Polish friend told me about an English language class he had. He said, "They gave me this list of words but didn't tell me what to do with them." Vygotsky helped me understand what to do with these new words of critical pedagogy; I had to hook them to thoughts.

The ideas of Vygotsky empowered my learning of the language and the thoughts of critical pedagogy. As I learned each new word or thought, new linkages would grow with my prior knowledge and existing experiential base. The most important lesson I learned from Vygotsky was that I had the ability to create new knowledge by using the relationship between thought and language.

Initially, I didn't even know the vocabulary, but I knew that I knew the ideas. Kids in schools had long ago taught me these same concepts. My experiences had brought me to the same place. I just didn't have the language to express what I was thinking. So, in order to even start, I had to learn the words. As I learned the words (in context) and played with the words, they gradually became mine. The words were sinking into the region of thought. Language finally began moving toward thought. Initially, these words were symbols without meaning; I had to play with them, read them, write them, talk about them, before gradually, meaning started to develop. The relationship between the words and the thought, however, is never static; as words develop, thought develops; and as thought gradually develops, the words change with the emerging ideas. I only hope that Nicolás and Micael listened to their mom.

In my particular case, the language of critical pedagogy, which at first had alienated, infuriated, and exasperated me, finally empowered me. From Vygotsky, I have learned that our words matter. Our words are not just neutral squiggles on paper. They are not just neutral symbols. Our language joins with our thoughts to generate meaning. As we increase our use of words, our thoughts deepen. The language we use matters. Sometimes language hurts one group of kids, and sometimes it helps another group.

Critical pedagogy forces educators to look again at the fundamental issues of power and their relationship to the greater societal forces that affect schools. *This comes dangerously close to being a definition!* Critical pedagogy has made me look again at the fundamental issues of power that are involved in the creation of a "trash" track. Critical pedagogy is forcing me to think and rethink my lived experiences as compared with those of my African American colleague. "Critical pedagogy asks how and why knowledge gets constructed the way it does, and how and why some constructions of reality are legitimated and celebrated by the dominant culture while others clearly are not" (McLaren, 1989, p. 169). For me, critical pedagogy is a new lens that enables me to see more clearly my past, my present, and my future.

One of the frustrating aspects of the study of critical pedagogy is our tendency to want others to transmit their knowledge of what it means to us. *"Just tell us what it means!"* During my initial encounters with these concepts, I was exactly like this. I felt angry, alienated, and excluded from this new knowledge. Repeatedly, I went to my professors to implore them to "just explain it." They repeatedly handed me another book. Each book triggered more questions.

Eventually, I came to the realization that I would have to find meaning for myself based on my own lived experiences. I do not believe that I can transmit my generated knowledge to you; however, I can share my story and in the process you can make your own connections based on your knowledge and experiences. This is not the *Cliff Notes of Critical Pedagogy*, but it is a collection of understandings about the language of critical pedagogy.

CONSCIENTIZATION

The truth is that I can barely pronounce the word *conscientization* in English, in Spanish, in Portuguese. I understand it. I know when I didn't have it. (When I was in Benson, I had *Hooked on Books*; I did not have conscientization.) I know when I began to develop it. (After teaching and learning with those Benson kids for a decade.) I know when teachers and learners have it. (Once Jonathan broke through the barrier of decoding, he had it because he knew that he knew.) I know when students don't have it. I recognize it when it is emerging in learners. I respect it. I understand its power. I love it. I just can't pronounce it very well. Not only that, it is extremely difficult to explain to others. It took me about two years of reading hard books before I really got it. So, if after reading this section, you don't feel as if you understand it, that's okay. Patience is fundamental to our learning. Courage is fundamental to our learning. Just keep reading and reflecting and talking and writing; soon you will come to understand its meaning based on your experiences.

Conscientization moves us from the passivity of "yeah-but-we-can't-do-that" to the power of "we-gotta-do-the-best-we-can-where-we-are-with-what-we've-got." For example, I see teachers as powerful humans who can make a difference in the lives of students. However, they often feel weak because they see themselves as victims of a system that renders them passive. Conscientization enables students and teachers to have confidence in their own knowledge, ability, and experiences. Often people will say that conscientization is a power we have when we recognize we *know* that we *know*.

In schools and communities, conscientization is knowing we know, and it is more. It means that we have voice and the courage to question ourselves and the role we are playing in maintaining educational processes that we do not value. Recently, at a faculty retreat, I watched a colleague explain that she was teaching a concept she knows has been discredited by further research. We asked her why she continued to maintain a process she cannot support. She needs to know that she knows; she needs conscientization; she needs courage to stop maintaining processes she knows do not work. Later, at the same retreat, another colleague spoke about a test he gives his students every semester. I know him, and I know this test. It is everything he doesn't believe in. I asked him why. Why does he continue to give this test if it flies in the face of his considerable knowledge and experience? Later, when he was presenting to the entire faculty, he mentioned the test and said he just realized he didn't know why he was giving it. I predict he won't next semester. Conscientization is emerging. He is coming to know that he knows. He is finding the power of his own voice, his own knowledge, his own experiences.

When I think of conscientization, I never think of a definition. I always think of people. Let me tell you a story of two teachers: One has conscientization and the other doesn't; well, she didn't.

Carmen Has It

I first met Carmen when she came to teach at a very low status, bilingual school in the South. I never could figure out why the district called this school the bilingual school; there was nothing bilingual about it. The teachers spoke English; the kids spoke Spanish. The teachers used English curriculum; the kids understood Spanish curriculum. I guess it was called the bilingual program because the Latino children went to school there. Until I met Carmen.

Carmen looked like a teacher who would be found in a Norman Rockwell painting. She had moved beyond the middle of life and had long salt-and-pepper hair pulled loosely into a topknot; small tendrils fell around her face. She had a slight build, with an air of strength and health about her. She looked very much like a woman who for many years had worked long hours and had eaten sparingly. Her clothes were a no-nonsense cotton that served her well in the classroom; her shoes were sturdy, as was her character. More than anything, one immediately noticed a sense of peace and purpose. She was courageous and patient. This was a woman who had known many teachers and many students and many parents; together they had been reading the world, reading the word (Freire & Macedo, 1987).

Eventually, I came to learn many things about Carmen and from Carmen. Carmen understood about learning, teaching, languages, literacies, cultures, knowledges. She had complex understandings and multiple perspectives. She thought kids needed to learn, so she taught in a language they understood: Spanish. In her class the students were continually generating language and ideas, language and ideas, language and ideas. I suspect she had read Vygotsky, too.

Carmen did not use the district-prescribed curriculum. She used the entire context of her students' lives for her curriculum. The state-mandated basals and materials served as just another resource to be used when needed. There were times when a certain activity viewed in isolation would appear to be much less than it actually was. Only the interaction of the entire context of her teaching could give full meaning to any activity.

For example, one day I walked into her class and noticed that Gilberto was, again, the center of attention. He was particularly adept at this, and I had come to think of him as Gilberto, the-most-frequent-office-visitor. Gilberto had recently gotten a new, very short haircut. He, in true Gilberto style, had arranged all day for his peers to be more interested in his new haircut than the lessons the teachers had planned. Already that morning I had heard a lot of grumbling from other teachers about him. However, there was something different about the kind of attention he was receiving in this class. Carmen and Gilberto were hand-in-hand walking behind each student's chair so that each had an opportunity to touch Gilberto's head. As they walked, Carmen was teaching the words and ideas: *brush, comb, shampoo, rinse, hot water, warm water, cool water.* Gilberto sat down, and Carmen wrote their language on the board. Together they created new thoughts and sentences with their generated language. Carmen wrote everything on the board. Teodoro mentioned that his hair felt ticklish. Carmen wrote *ticklish* on the board, and the students read the word and giggled. Soon all the children had their own journals on their desks and were busy using their language to write new sentences. Carmen knew the importance of including the children and their world in her lessons. After this particular lesson, Carmen walked across the hall to Rainey's classroom.

Carmen knew the power of Gilberto and his new haircut; and, she *knew* that she *knew*: conscientization. She also knew that Rainey, a beginning teacher, who worked with the same group of children for their English language development and their math and science, would need a little push in this direction, or she would have continued with her prescribed lesson on the colors in English. The children would have memorized those lists of words, but as the Polish student taught us, they wouldn't have known what to do with them. Carmen knew how to make those words and ideas work for her students. Carmen soon had Rainey and the students busily involved with funny new words in English—words like *ticklish, prickly, spike, flattop*—words that never would have been on the English-as-a-Second-Language (ESL) list for memorizing.

Carmen and Gilberto had created an activity that mattered to the kids. Every minute was used for the learning and teaching process. In this classroom, Freire (cited in McLaren, 1989) would not find a "culture of silence." The children were not silent because they felt less or were afraid; they were silent only when it was meaningful in their learning. At the end of the day, each child had written a story, using all of their new words and ideas, about funny new haircuts.

Carmen, more than any other teacher, taught me the power of conscientization in the practice of her class. She knew her beliefs from years of experiences and books and ideas and people. She turned her beliefs into behaviors in every moment of her life. Her students grew to love themselves; their teachers grew to love the students; the students grew into their own biliteracy; and the power of this pulled the community into the process. The peace and purpose that was Carmen transformed the students, her colleagues, and their students. As you read this book, please don't memorize a definition; just remember Carmen. In addition, reflect on someone you know who has conscientization, and please reflect on your own.

Conscientization is . . .

The person I know who has conscientization is . . .
because . . .

In my own personal development of conscientization, I would say
that I . . .

Rainey Doesn't; Well, Didn't

Rainey was as vivacious as Carmen was private. Rainey taught in English; Carmen taught in Spanish. Rainey had never been around Mexican kids; she continually complained to me about them and their behavior. Carmen had always been around Mexican kids; she continually told me how smart and loving they were. Rainey was new to teaching; Carmen was not. The first time I met Rainey in school, she desperately implored, "Okay, I've taught the weather in English—now, what do I do?" The first time I met Carmen, she matter-of-factly told me that I would need to get her some more books in a language the students could understand. It would be safe to say that Rainey did not have conscientization. Carmen did.

Rainey: BC. Let me describe some of Rainey's *behaviors before conscientization* and *before Carmen (BC)*. The following is a list of things she said about her students at the beginning of the year:

Ollie: One of the worst.
Gilberto: A terrible problem.
Carlos: Ugh.
María and Irma: Pitiful sisters.
Cristina: Doesn't know anything.

The meetings with the families provided multiple opportunities to observe her behaviors, which told me much about her beliefs. Rainey would enter the school auditorium with a smile on her face, walk to the front row without speaking to any of the families, bury herself in the middle of the first row, where she was safely surrounded by the other teachers, and cross her arms. Several empty rows of auditorium seats always provided a safe buffer between the parents and the teachers. Rainey and many of her colleagues came from a tradition of family involvement that assumed teachers would talk; families would listen. The purpose of this approach to family involvement is to change the families. Rainey subscribed to this thinking, but that was BC.

Rainey: AC. Within a few short months, the power of Carmen began to work its magic. Rainey changed *after Carmen* and *after conscientization* (AC). When she came to the family meetings, she would arrive with a smile on her face and walk up to all the families and use her limited Spanish. They warmed to her approach and were more than willing to teach her more. Her use of their language grew. Soon, she was visiting with so many family members as she entered the meetings that she could never make it to the safe front row of the auditorium. I began to find her in the middle of the parents wherever they were sitting. Rainey came to appreciate a new approach to family involvement. Instead of doing something to them, she came to understand why she should do things with them. Instead of trying to change the parents, she was soon trying to change the school.

Once, she and Carmen were discussing family involvement and what the families needed. Rainey suggested to Carmen that she could go to the university library and do a computer search to find out. Carmen nodded and added, "Or, we could ask the families." At the next family meeting, the teachers asked, and the families told them their needs.

The Families' Needs

more family meetings
a written copy of the teacher's schedule
an understanding of the assigned homework
more time with their children
less time with TV

Rainey and Carmen chuckled during the meeting as they thought about Rainey going to the library instead of just asking the parents.

Another example of Rainey: AC happened about the same time. The results of initiating and implementing a parent advisory committee are not often visible immediately, but they are worth the wait. Carmen always went to visit in the homes of her students. This was a very frightening thought for Rainey, and she resisted for months. Finally, she went to visit in the home of Carlos, one of her students who previously had almost convinced her to leave the teaching profession because of his behavior.

One day I was walking down a corridor in this school and realized that I was looking at Rainey and Carlos as they leaned on their elbows and stared out the window toward the playground; their bodies made dark silhouettes against the sunlight. Their heads were about an inch apart, and they were both facing the playground. By the slow movement of their heads, I could see that they were quietly visiting. I backed down the hall so as not to disturb them.

Rainey, BC, thought Carlos was the worst; she physically grimaced every time his name was mentioned. She and other teachers used to talk about him in the faculty lounge. I used to try to imagine how terrible it would be to be in the first grade when all of those in authority were against me.

As I watched Rainey and Carlos talk quietly and stare out the window, I remembered how she used to talk about him; now she was visiting with him. Rainey thought that Carlos had changed. I think that Rainey has changed.

I remember Rainey telling me about the home visit. She was astounded to discover that he had a good home environment, with a loving and supportive family; his brothers and sisters were successful in school. She was relieved to learn that Carlos's mom shared her concern for Carlos. The mother could not understand why Carlos wasn't learning at the same pace as his brothers and sisters, Carlos's mom was too uncomfortable and alienated to come to the school and discuss her concerns.

Rainey told me that before the visit, she assumed that Carlos' behavior was a result of his home. She assumed that the child, the child's family, and the child's culture were the principle causes of his failure. After the home visit, she began to work with his mom to understand him, and his behavior immediately improved. Carlos is a different person when he is with Rainey.

However, Rainey still has a critical step to take. She still thinks that Carlos has changed. She needs to critically examine herself and her environment and come to the realization that she is a part of the process of transformation. In Carlos's search for knowledge and literacy, she is a significant variable. I like to think that if Paulo Freire had been with me in that hall, he would have told me that this was conscientization: a transformation of the learner and teacher as a result of interaction between the two of them.

I'm not worried about Rainey. If she can move this far toward an intercultural orientation in the time that I have known her, soon she will *know* that she *knows*, and she will go on to help others read the world and read the word (Freire & Macedo, 1987).

Rainey: BC

Before Carmen
Before Conscientization
Before Carlos

Rainey: AC

After Carmen
After Conscientization
After Carlos

CODIFICATION

Codification is the concept, captured on paper, in the dirt, on the chalkboard, on the wall. It is the thought, painted. It is the symbol, symbolized. I have known teachers to codify thoughts in pictures, in action, in clay, in paint. I always visualize Paulo Freire, before he was banished from Brazil for developing literacy among the native peoples, standing in the shade of a tree codifying with a stick in the dirt the powerful ideas of rage and oppression that the workers were expressing. I have no idea if he stood in the shade, and I have no idea if he ever used a stick to draw in the dirt, but this is the image I carry with me to make meaning of codification. I have to tell you that I think Freire was on to something with this idea of codification. It captures the best of many powerful approaches to teaching and learning. It brings in the students' world and builds knowledges and literacies based on their own unique experiences. It puts the power back into teaching and learning. And, it integrates the never-ending debate between *doing* and *living* critical pedagogy.

Remember Jonathan and his board, and the tongues, and the throats, and the tiny sounds: lip popper, lip tappers, and so on? Remember that I thought I didn't like it? Remember it opened the door for Jonathan? Could it be that it was a type of codification that was necessary for Jon's ways of knowing? For Jon, the concept was finally captured.

> Codes (or "codifications" in Freire's terms) are concrete physical expressions that combine all the elements of the theme into one representation. They can take many forms: photographs, drawings, collages, stories, written dialogues, movies, songs. Codes are more than visual aids for teaching. They are at the heart of the educational process because they initiate critical thinking.
>
> No matter what the form, code is a projective device that is emotionally laden and identifiable to students. . . . In essence, a code sums up or "codifies" into one statement a problem (or contradiction) that people recognize in their lives: need for English vs. loss of native culture, stress at work vs. need for work, disappointment vs. hope from expectations in the U.S. Each problem is complex without narrowly defined good and bad sides.
>
> After a problem or contradiction has been coded, we can begin to "decode" it—we can begin to unravel it or find workable solutions. (Wallerstein, 1983, pp. 19–20)

Critical pedagogy forces us to see the broad social, historical, cultural, and political context of teaching and learning. *Critical pedagogy* gives us the courage to say what we see. *Critical pedagogy* is grounded in justice, equity, and moral mandates. *Critical pedagogy* makes us ask fundamental questions: What is the right thing to do today in my teaching and learning in this particular context? It is as broad as the world and as deep as our own individual lives. *Critical pedagogy* makes us look at the world, and it makes us look at our individual role in the world, the community, the classroom. *Critical pedagogy* is like a lens that enables us to see more clearly, more critically, more keenly.

CULTURAL CAPITAL

Cultural capital refers to the behaviors, values, and practices that are valued by the dominant society.

Dawn worried that other teachers made disparaging remarks because her kindergarten students would not stand in a straight line. Although she was intuitively opposed to five-year-olds standing in a straight line, she could see their failure to do so was having a negative effect on her students. When she said "forménse," they would gather in a circle around her, arms around each other, look at her, and smile. She thought that it looked like a group hug. The other teachers thought that it looked like unruly, poorly behaved Mexican kids.

She decided to teach them to stand in line so they could have cultural capital. She told them to get in line and put their hands on the shoulders of the person in front of each of them. They dissolved into giggles as they tried to choke and to tickle each other. She took them to the basketball court and told them to walk on the line, where they tiptoed as if on a high wire. In the classroom they lined up sticks, rocks, blocks, pencils, and papers. Finally, they went outside to wait for the buses. "Forménse," she said. They immediately formed the best straight line. The other teachers began to smile approvingly.

When Dawn was in kindergarten, she had lots of cultural capital. She knew what was socially and culturally expected in the environment of school. She knew how to get into line, to keep her hands to herself, and to be quiet at certain times. She didn't always do it, but she knew. Now, as a teacher, Dawn discovered that her students had little cultural capital, and they were blamed for it.

Dawn still struggles with this because she prefers the group hug.

Cultural capital is a process of powerful practices: ways of behaving, talking, acting, thinking, moving, and so forth. These practices are determined unconsciously by the dominant culture and are used to promote success for specific groups in our society.

For example, in North American businesses and educational institutions, it is believed that we must speak in a very direct and concise manner to succeed. This manner of speaking is gender-specific and culturally laden; European American men like to speak this way, and they like others to speak this way. These high-status speech patterns carry value and carry men to the top. This linear-speak is valued by the power structures in North America, but this is not true in much of the world. Many cultural groups find that it provides a limited context, and they prefer to speak in a more enriched contextual frame. Much of the world (including some North American women) prefer to tell stories to make a point; they prefer to provide many perspectives and variables because they believe listeners (or readers) will generate meaning based on their own lived experiences.

Often the nondominant culture buys into the dominant culture's way of thinking; they support it and encourage it. For example, when women began moving into the upper ranks of business, some women wore business suits that looked very much like men's business suits. Some women tried to *look like* men so they could move ahead professionally. More recently, women seem to feel freer to dress like women. However, sometimes women still support more subtle forms of cultural capital. Their business suits may be gone, but often their linear-speak is still bouncing around the offices. A very bright young businesswoman recently told me that "you have to talk like men in order to get ahead." I am confident that there are many powerful and effective ways of speaking. The dominant society uses cultural capital to lure the nondominant groups into being like them. Nondominant people often are recruited for diversity, and then powerful dominant forces try to change their ways of knowing and being.

Sometimes cultural capital varies from region to region. I remember an 80+-year-old man, Mr. Tom, talking to me about his brother. Mr. Tom lived on a ranch on the prairies and placed much value on all that ranchers know about cattle. His brother had recently retired from a brilliant career as a Boeing engineer, but Mr. Tom dismissed his knowledge with one concise statement: "He doesn't know a damn thing about cows."

DIALECTIC

A *dialectic* is the tension of *yining* and *yanging* (the backing and forthing) of thoughts, ideas, values, beliefs. A dialectic is occurring as I write this chapter on definitions. I know readers feel *just-tell-me-what-it-means*, and I am feeling *just-discover-what-it-means*. This is a dialectic. I know that definitions can be very helpful along the unlearning curve, but I am terrified that someone will take them and memorize them. Please, please, please don't memorize these definitions. Please, please, please don't fall into the jargon pit. Definitions have value only if the reader sits, reads, reflects, connects, and muses on them.

A dialectic is what happens when you are sitting in a class, a presentation, an inservice. You have been talked at, talked at, and talked at. You can barely sit still because you have a different perspective; you understand in a totally other way. You want to jump up and share your thoughts and hear the thoughts of those sitting near you. Suddenly the presenter stops and asks the participants to discuss in small groups. The "backing-and-forthing" of ideas breaks out in each small group. This is good.

Let me share with you another dialectic that I live daily. I have many wonderful books. My books are my treasures and are personalized with family pictures, beautiful cards, pictures of authors, and cartoons that relate to the text. If you send me a card, I will tape it to the front of a book with a wide piece of transparent tape, and I will always think of you when I grab that book. The truth is that my books are really quite spectacular. I love them, and the students love them. I love to share them, and I hate to share them. Therefore, I am in a constant dialect—with myself. Every time I go to class, I try not to carry my books and tell about authors and ideas, but, I am really quite helpless. I love my books so much that I can't help myself. I know if I tell students about the books and ideas and authors, they will want to read my books. This is what I want and don't want. I want to share the books, and I hate to share the books. I don't want my books on my shelves, and I want my books on my shelves. As so many grad students have families and major financial responsibilities, I try not to require texts, only to recommend. They can read my books. Of course, I do more damage than good, because they borrow and end up loving books, too, and eventually buy more than I would ever require. Every year I am short a few books, which I don't really mind, as I feel they probably have a good home and are being loved by someone else. I continue to yin and yang with my books: I want to share; I don't want to share; I want to share; I don't want to share.

I am noticing that technology people are the same way. They want us to connect, and they don't want us to connect. They are happy that we are using a modem, and they are mad that we are filling up the modem pool. They want us to love the great Internet of the sky, and they worry that we will love it too much.

Paulo Freire talks about the dialectic of being "patiently impatient" (cited in Gadotti, 1994, p. 47). A dialectic involves seeing and articulating contradictions; it is the process of learning from the oppositional view. Jonathan has provided a dialectical learning experience for me. A dialectic brings to light a more comprehensive understanding of the multiple facets of "the opposite." As we learn while teaching and teach while learning, we are in a dialectical process. Other dialectics mentioned in this book are:

> *courage and patience*
> *a caring heart and a critical eye*

DIALOGUE

Dialogue is change-agent chatter. *Dialogue* is talk that changes us or our context. *Dialogue* is profound, wise, insightful conversation. *Dialogue* is two-way, interactive visiting. *Dialogue* involves periods of lots of noise as people share and lots of silence as people muse. *Dialogue* is communication that creates and recreates multiple understandings. It moves its participants along the learning curve to that uncomfortable place of relearning and unlearning. It can move people to wonderful new levels of knowledge; it can transform relations; it can change things.

We visit with someone, and our world changes for the better. For example, a high-status, wealthy woman in a local community has been writing letters to the editor of the local newspaper, speaking to the school board, speaking to administrators, and circulating a petition. Her cause is to redo the reading and language arts program in the local schools. I have questions: How much does she really know about languages? literacies? cultures? knowledges? However, I have been so busy working on this book and trying to stay ahead of my students that I haven't done what I should have. I haven't called her to hear what she has to say; I haven't had a dialogue with her.

One of my friends, though, who is a teacher in the local schools, did make time to call and enter into a little change-agent chatter. The dialogue of the two women demonstrates that they are generating knowledge and coming to understand together. They are discovering meaning as they visit. Their talk matters and will eventually have a significant effect on many students. The two women have known each other for many years; their children were in pre-K programs together. These two women have shared experiences. After their dialogue, they wrote letters to each other. I am including one of these letters as a sample of the dynamic nature of dialogue (see Figure 2.1).

This letter, which was written by my teacher friend, was a follow-up to their initial dialogue. After they had spoken with each other and written letters to each other, the first woman withdrew her petition and acknowledged that she had acted with misinformation. I will be watching this situation closely, as I suspect this ongoing dialogue will have wider ramifications for children. When she and my teacher friend join together there is a great potential for powerful change.

DISCOURSE

Remember when discourse was . . . well, what in the world was it?

FIGURE 2.1   A letter arising from the dialogue
Dear Sally,

I received your letter yesterday. I must tell you how respectful I am of the courage this entire procedure has shown you to have. You should never be regretful for voicing a concern and taking action on that belief. That takes courage. I never saw the petition, so I don't know what it says. I heard there was a concern from you. Our shared past history told me that you weren't a hurtful or vengeful person. If you had a concern, it had to be well thought out. I called because I was interested in your opinion. I still am. As you pointed out, people working and talking together can create change and more understanding between opposite philosophies. Sally, you opened the door. We need to make sure that the opportunity for dialogue does not close. I talked with the district personnel about some more public forums for parents to discuss concerns. You were/are exactly right about dialogue.

I would like to invite you to a small group of professionals who meet monthly. We get together to discuss holistic teaching and learning, read books and discuss them, and generally support one another.

The more I learn about education, the more I understand that I have much to learn. As a late starter, it is my job and my avocation. I love what I do. New ideas cause me great excitement. For many teachers, however, I suspect that this type of joy is gone. For me, change is acceptable and challenging. With our body of knowledge expanding daily, life is not going to be the same as 10 years ago. And, 10 years from now, it may be unrecognizable in terms of education. Alvin Toffler, the futurist says,

> The illiterate of the future are not those who can't read and write but those who cannot learn, unlearn, and relearn.

You can see why I believe in dialogue. Without it, learning, unlearning, and re-learning won't happen. Change is scary. The unlearn/relearn process is new ground. Whenever we change our minds about something, we are involved in the unlearn/relearn at some point along the continuum. I think that anyone on that continuum is exhibiting courage. Your courage to change is an example. I hope we can continue to dialogue.

Sincerely,

Donna

Perhaps we remember discourse as something that was studied with rhetoric in college? Something more serious and more important than a discussion? Interaction? Something that carried status and power and was somehow related to profound speeches?

It turns out that *discourse* is not just the use of words. Rather, it is the use of loaded words that establish who is on which rung of the ladder. And, it turns out that there are lots of ladders, or discourses. *Discourses* reflect a certain place; they are all socially and culturally grounded. For example, I am not at home with the discourse of statistics; I can do it and talk it and think it, but the truth is, I am just not at home with that particular discourse. In fact, when I find myself in that place, I have been known to invent language to make meaning of that context. I have a friend, Debe, who thrives on the discourse of statistics; I think she talks funny, and she thinks I talk funny in that environment. We both see and know in very different ways when it comes to the discourse of statistics. She is central to a group of my friends who love statistics; I am "the other." On that ladder she is several rungs above me.

Today discourse can sound like dialogue, only in *discourse,* the words carry subtle (and not so subtle) messages about power. It seeks to establish the hidden rules for who speaks and who listens; what knowledge is good and bad; whose words have more power and whose words are marginalized.

As I reflect back to 30 years ago, it seems that the meaning has changed—yet another change. I remember my first conscious experience with discourse. I don't remember what it meant, but I remember the professor who taught the class; I remember his name, his class, his walk, his eyes. I remember the fear we felt in the class. I remember reading, and reading and writing, and having to enter into discourse in the class. I remember how passionately he felt about discourse; it mattered to him. As the semester and nervous stomachaches continued, I remember I began to feel more confident, more important, (dare I say it?) more elite. I had status and privilege. I think the word *discourse* for him was more in line with rhetoric and oratory. As I reflect on the unspoken feelings of that class, I can now see that even then the messages we received were filled with messages of power and lack of power. Through this vehicle of the discourse class, we were assigned status, power, and prestige. I was rewarded for my conformity with an "A." I hope the meaning of discourse has changed!

The power of discourse, or disempowerment in this case, can been seen in the use of the word, *limited.* To label any student *limited* is to limit how that student is institutionally perceived; how that student feels about her capabilities and potential; how peers feel about that student. To articulate the various levels of limitations is to socially sort students' status, as can been seen in the following class filled with teachers.

The graduate class had several discussions about the hidden language we all use to produce and reproduce social status and power. We had focused on words such as LEP *[limited English proficient],* LES *[limited English speaker],* GATE *[Gifted and Talented Education],* challenged, disadvantaged, at-risk, minority, *and so forth. We had recently learned of a school with a program for "potential dropouts." After much discussion, we had agreed that to place a student in this program would send a negative message regarding our expectations for the student. The class held a dialogue about the importance of critically reflecting on our own language; therefore, we were all a little surprised at the following discourse, which unexpectedly emerged in class.*

We were discussing how assessment of bilingual children often does not lead to programs that serve the needs of these students.

"But, in our school we even have two levels of ESL instruction. One section is for the high-limiteds, and the other class is for the low-limiteds," a graduate student proudly told us. "I teach the low-limiteds."

Silence hung in the room, as we internalized the meaning of discourse.

Recently, a conversation with a friend/colleague provided an unexpected opportunity to reflect and act on the importance of discourse. As professionals, our language does make a difference, as seen in the following conversation. My colleague and I had been discussing the third colleague, whose annual evaluation had not been favorable.

JOAN: Do the written evaluations indicate that he has had any successful experiences with students?

T: Oh, yes, he does okay with normal students.

JOAN: With normal students? Who would that be?

T: Well, okay, I mean with regular students.

JOAN: With regular students? And, who would that be?

T: Well, okay, what word do you want me to use?

JOAN: I don't know. Use an adjective. Who are you talking about?

T: Okay, I mean with Anglo, English-only students.

My colleague recognized the power of language. By labeling one group *normal* and *regular*, other groups in our program immediately were marginalized. This is how the norm is normalized, the regular is regularized, the standard is standardized. For professors to use this type of discourse, no matter how innocently, is to lower the value of one group of students and to raise the value of another.

This point was recognized by another teacher in the area in a story that she shared:

> *I was visiting with another teacher who wanted to know why students who come from other countries often cross the numeral 7 with a bar in the middle. I explained that they were clarifying the difference between a number 7 and a number 1. She nodded her head in understanding. She then wondered why they use a front tail on the number 1. I answered that it was to clarify the difference between a number 1 and a lowercase letter l. She realized that some of her students did confuse the number 1 and the lowercase l because of the North American style of writing. However, she ended our discussion by saying, "Why can't they just do it the normal way?"*

Joining the Prairie Club

My family, friends, and I have been spending quite of bit of time on our ranch on the plains lately. This has provided many opportunities to think about being admitted to the discourse of the prairies. We immediately know when we are admitted membership and when we are denied membership. Dean, my husband, is gaining entrance into the Prairie Club because he looks like the other members of the club. He wears the same clothes, knows about cows, and has the same one-finger wave as he passes lonely trucks on the highway. He is hardier than the average, friendlier than the average, and taller than the average. When he speaks with the Prairie Club members, he uses the same quiet, reserved language that establishes credibility and respect. Slowly, the doors of the Prairie Club are swinging open, and he is being granted admission. The Club will affect him, and he will affect the Club.

Recently, California friends came to visit on the ranch in January. Never mind that they are the antithesis of every California stereotype, it was clear that the locals resisted allowing them to join the discourse of the rural and isolated plains. I noticed that my neighbors, with a twinkle in their eyes, would periodically ask how our California friends were enjoying the midwestern winter. It was clear that the hardy plains natives assumed that the California couple was suffering, which provided a little entertainment for the charter members of the Prairie Club, too. Our California friends always responded simply and positively to questions about the cold weather, but it remained obvious that the Club members were reserving discourse membership for only the natives.

On one particular day, it was 0 degrees and the wind was blowing. The wind chill factor was probably 30 degrees below zero, and the howl of the wind created a forlorn sound across the prairies. My friend Sharon went with us in the cattle truck to feed the cows. En route to feed, we stopped to visit with some neighbors in the small grocery store/post office, which is the heart and soul of the Prairie Club. As Sharon blew through the front door, all eyes were on her. The store owner said what the others were thinking:

> *"Well, what do you think of this weather?"*
> *"Sure is crisp," Sharon calmly responded, slowly drawing out the sound of each consonant. A moment of silence hung in the air as the Prairie Club members stared at her and mused on how to handle this most acceptable, stoic, and understated response. Finally, the store owner, a high-status, respected member of the ranch discourse community said, "Yes, you are right. It sure is crisp."*

With that brief discourse, Sharon was granted preliminary membership to this particular rural discourse community. Now, if she had said, "Whoa! It is so cold that I'm ready to return to the sunny coast," the door to membership in the discourse of ranches would have slammed shut permanently (see Note 2).

HEGEMONY

Hegemony is the domination of one group over another with the partial consent of the dominated group. It is the control of knowledge and literacy by the dominant group. In the following scene, a high school teacher shares with us how one type of cultural knowledge was affirmed and validated in her presence and another type of cultural knowledge was denigrated.

> *"Rap music and break dancing are not allowed at our school," Mr. Smith, the principal, announced as he stormed into my classroom. He grabbed B.J. by the ear, literally pulling him out of the class. I was not physically strong enough to prevent him from dragging B.J. out of class and down the hall. I turned my attention back to the other students. After they were settled and working on their assignments, I walked down to Mr. Smith's office to check on B.J.*
> *"B.J. has been suspended. He has broken our rules. Perhaps this will set an example for the rest of the students that we set the rules, and when we do, we mean business," Mr. Smith told me. I just walked back to class shaking my head, but I couldn't help but reflect on the fact that Mr. Smith's (elevator) music was playing in the office of this school, which was located in the middle of the African American community in town.*

To be completely true to a definition of hegemony, B.J. would partially have to support Mr. Smith's action. We could say that B.J. began to reject rap music in favor of elevator music. The truth is, that didn't happen. However, B.J. did get very angry and is now considered a *problem* in school.

Enriched programs can be used as a hegemonic tool to groom one group and to marginalize and silence another. The following conversation between a school secretary and a director of assessment took place in the front office of an elementary school.

> *"This is a request for an assessment for the gifted program," the secretary said to the director.*
> *"Really? Who for?" the director of assessment responded.*
> *"José."*
> *"A minority in Gifted? Those tests are in English. He doesn't know anything," the director said with a dismissing wave of her hand.*

HIDDEN CURRICULUM

The *hidden curriculum* is the unexpressed perpetuation of dominant culture through institutional processes. McLaren (1998, Summer, p. 45) calls it the pedagogical unsaid. The *hidden curriculum* is covert and insidious, and only a critical lens will bring it into view. It teaches what is assumed to be important. It defines the standard for the dominant culture. Critical pedagogy asks: Whose standard? Whose culture? Whose knowledge? Whose history? Whose language? Whose perspective? Critical pedagogy seeks to make pluralism plural: standards, cultures, knowledges, histories, languages, perspectives. Society has a tendency to domesticate students into believing the dominant view. Sometimes, it is supported by those who are marginalized by the hidden processes because (a) they haven't taken time to reflect critically on themselves and their roles or (b) it is seen, cynically, as the superhighway that must be used to get ahead.

Sometimes, the hidden curriculum becomes such a part of the curriculum that no one notices it. For example, Vicky teaches in the Northwest. She is located in a very rural area that has a history populated by Native Americans, their culture, their language, and their ways of knowing. When she started teaching the junior high students, she noticed that the history of the local Native Americans was never studied nor mentioned. The week before Thanksgiving, she asked a Native American eighth-grade boy what Thanksgiving was all about, and his response was, "The white man taught the savages how to plant." The room, filled with European Americans and Native American students, nodded in agreement. Only Vicky, the teacher, realized the devastating nature of the hidden curriculum.

The hidden curriculum can been seen in schools when little boys are called on more than little girls; when only Eurocentric histories are taught; when teenage girls are socialized to believe that they are not good in math and sciences; when heroes, and not heroines, are taught; when counselors track nonwhites to classes that prepare them to serve.

LITERACIES

Remember when literacy was reading and writing? Remember when we thought it was simple? Turns out, we were wrong. Perhaps our traditional assumptions of literacy were not only simple, but maybe even simplistic. The world has changed. Schools have changed. Students have changed. Now, we are coming to know multiple types of literacies: *functional* (languages of the streets and of life); *academic* (languages of schools and universities); *workplace* (languages of our jobs); *information* (languages of technology); *constructive* (languages we construct with the printed word); *emergent* (languages constructed with the text before we are really decoding); *cultural* (language that reflects the perspective of one culture—guess which one?); and *critical* (languages that take us deeper into more complex understandings of the word and the world); and, finally, *literacies* as a new type of literacy that provides a foundation reflective of multiple experiences. Literacies are reading, writing, and reflecting. Literacies help us make sense of our world and do something about it.

I should have known literacy would be more complex than my traditional assumptions. I have watched many students develop (and not develop) their literacies in multiple ways. Jonathan is just one of the kids who has forced me to expand my understandings of literacy to be far more inclusive of all types of literacies.

All these literate processes have one common characteristic: They all are derived from social practices. Literacies are socially constructed often with our friends, in specific contexts, for specific purposes. Literacies do not develop in isolation; rather, literate processes grow from families, from schools, from work, from cultures, from knowledges, from technologies, and so on.

If the new and more complex meanings of literacies begin to slip away from you, go back to the section on *Discourses* and start again. It is a very similar concept. Debe was one to frolic in and relish every level, every facet, every dimension, every implication of the literacies of statistics. On the other hand, my literacy in that world could never have been considered plural, it was barely singular, which reflects my tiny understanding of statistics. Do not be fooled into thinking that the term *literacies* is just specific vocabulary for one particular context. It is not. It is the underlying ways of knowing, thinking, and making complex meanings. Each of us brings our own world when learning to read the word and reread the world. I thank Jim Cummins (1998, March 20) for reminding me of Moffett's critical definition of literacy:

> Literacy is dangerous and has always been so regarded. It naturally breaks down barriers of time, space, and culture. It threatens one's original identity by broadening it through vicarious experiencing and the incorporation of somebody else's hearth and ethos. So we feel profoundly ambiguous about literacy. Looking at it as a means of transmitting our culture to our children, we give it priority in education, but recognizing the threat of its backfiring we make it so tiresome and personally unrewarding that youngsters won't want to do it on their own, which is of course when it becomes dangerous. . . . The net effect of this ambivalence is to give literacy with one hand and take it back with the other, in keeping with our contradictory wish for youngsters to learn to think but only about what we already have in mind for them. (Moffett, 1989, p. 85)

In the introduction to this edition, I mentioned how the world has changed since the first edition. This is an example. I muse on this 1989 quotation, and I wonder how Moffett knew what was coming ten years ahead of his time?

Reading the Word and the World

Yes, *critical literacy* is reading and writing, but it's much, much more (see Note 3). *Critical literacy* involves knowing, lots of knowing. It also involves seeing, lots of seeing. It enables us to read the social practices of the world all too clearly. *Critical literacy* can push us into the zone of all-this-learning-really-isn't-so-great. *Critical literacy* means that we understand how and why knowledge and power are constructed and by whom and for whom:

> ### Reading the Word means
> to decode/encode those words;
>
> to bring ourselves to those pages;
>
> to make meaning of those pages as they relate to our experiences, our possibilities; our cultures; and our knowledges.

Reading the World means
to decode/encode the people around us;
to decode/encode the community that surrounds us;
to decode/encode the visible and invisible messages of the world.

Traditionally, literacy has been Reading the Word (to paraphrase Freire and Macedo's title) or decoding sounds and letters. *Critical literacy* is Reading the World, or encoding the power structures and our role in these processes (Freire & Macedo, 1987). *Critical literacy* (see Note 4) recognizes that reading does not take place in a vacuum; it includes the entire social, cultural, political, and historical context. In what follows, I introduce you to a variety of people who have sadly read the world.

Many five-year-olds do this before they ever enter school. From TV, their family, trips to the store, they understand power. They read who speaks and who listens, where, and when, and to whom.

> *Five-year-old, José and his family nervously entered the school for the first time. They found the office and entered to begin the enrollment process. The secretary greeted them in English and handed them a packet of papers, all of which were written only in English.*
>
> *"Fill out these papers, please," she said to José and his family. As they looked nervously at the papers, Jane, the secretary, walked from around the counter, took José by the hand and walked out in the hallway. En route to a kindergarten class, she was joined by two teachers.*
>
> *"Whose class will he be in?" one of them asked.*
>
> *"Put him in Special Ed. He's from Mexico; he doesn't know anything," the other replied.*
>
> *Defeated and with his head down, José entered the classroom.*

José cannot yet read the word, but he has read the world very clearly. José started school the same day as Carmen, his teacher. Together, Carmen and José taught me many things, including the meaning of critical literacy. It was not long before José was engaged actively in reading and learning with Carmen in her classroom.

Chris, a young African American man, remembers when he was 5 years old and he learned to read the world.

> *When I was in kindergarten, I used to love to play with my friend, Peggy. She was European American, and I was African but we*

had not yet discovered that it mattered. All we knew was that we loved to swing and slide during recess. She was my best friend. One day she ran up to me and said, "You're black." She slapped me across the face and ran away. I remember crying. Later, when I went home, I told my Dad. I could tell that he was very sad when he taught me to read the world.

Orate and Literate Communities

We in North America put much faith in literate communities. We place high status on literacy, or reading and writing. Status and prestige are not assigned to those who are *illiterate*, a word that carries heavy connotations of *less*. *Illiteracy* has become a loaded, value-laden concept that is used to deny access to power. For example, when we say, "They are illiterate," we often mean much more than they are not able to decode. However, this is not true in much of the world (Skutnabb-Kangas, 1993). Many people in the world carry their knowledge in their head and not on paper. Important people carry important knowledge in their heads. Instead of being literate communities, these are called orate communities.

Jonathan has lots of orate knowledge, although he still struggles with those spelling tests. However, his computer spell-check makes that irrelevant. His orate knowledge is highly relevant. Another example is a mariachi guitar player I knew. He carried the entire history of the Mexican revolution in his head, and he could sing and play it. After taking lessons from him, I learned the difference between orate and literate communities. I now have boxes and boxes of Mexican music with all the verses that I have transcribed from the tapes I made of him singing. These boxes are dusty and in my garage. His orate knowledge is still in his head.

So much of our knowledge serves us better when we carry it in our heads, and not on paper. For example, when I am in the grocery store, at the dinner table, at a coffee lounge, and people ask me questions about education, or multilingual education, or critical literacy, they don't want me to get out my papers, my books, my transparencies and answer their questions. They just want me to tell them in plain language something that is understandable.

If you are a teacher, there is a fun way to learn about orate and literate communities with your students. Start your class by explaining that for today, the time will be spent doing a big review of all that has been learned. Tell your students they will need a blank piece of paper. Watch carefully what their do; they will immediately begin looking for papers with notes, for books, for old journals—in any place where the knowledge is contained. Tell them: No, no, no. Use your brain; just brains, no books, no notes, no charts, no index cards. Just brains. Just orate literacy. Begin your review with some leading questions of what has been studied. You and the students will learn together that much of our knowledge is not carried in our heads; it's in our books and we only access it. I suspect there is a lot we could learn from orate people who are often referred to as *illiterates*.

PEDAGOGY

Pedagogy is the interaction between teaching and learning. I used to think that pedagogy was only about teaching: how I taught; what I taught; and why I taught it. I thought pedagogy was a vehicle by which I drove ideas into the heads of students. I thought that if I taught in the "right" way, my pedagogy would be "perfect" and obviously the students would learn "perfectly." At least that is what I thought until I starting teaching. You can well imagine my shock to discover that the students had more to teach me. Pedagogy is not just about me, teaching. *Pedagogy* is the process of teaching and learning together. It is fundamentally about human interactions (see Note 5), the joy of playing with new ideas, and the challenge of integrating those ideas in the real world.

PRAXIS

These stories are my praxis. My theory and my practice have joined together in the creation of the stories in this book. The stories reflect practice in classrooms that is grounded in theory. The theory is to be discovered in the practice. The stories reflect how beliefs become behaviors in the classroom, and how we can reflect on our beliefs by critically examining our behaviors. I am one of those teachers who focused on only practice for many years. I didn't even realize that in those years of teaching, I was building theory. It was only after I went back to graduate school that I discovered, to my great joy, that there were books about what my students had been teaching me for years. To this day, I see former students' faces when I read theory, talk about theory, reflect on theory. I came to theory through practice. Some do it the other way around.

Praxis is the constant reciprocity of our theory and our practice. Theory building and critical reflection inform our practice and our action, and our practice and action inform our theory building and critical reflection.

This semester I am teaching a methods course that is designed to assist English-dominant teachers who are working in a multilingual context. We focus on methods, on practice, and on the how-to, even though it is hard for me. After years of practicing practice, my bias is now on theory. The *why* is more interesting to me than the *how*. However, this is a methods course, and we practice various methods. One night in class, I slipped in a little why, and the students seemed very responsive. After class, a teacher was walking out and said to me, "A little theory never hurts." Yes, I thought, and a little practice never hurts. That is what praxis is: practice grounded in theory and theory grounded in practice.

PROBLEM POSING

Problem posing is much more than just a method, or a series of methods. My purpose here is to generate a definition or a description of problem posing, which is central to teaching and learning critically. Jonathan is an example of difficult problem posing for me. *Problem posing* brings interactive participation and critical inquiry into the existing curriculum and expands it to reflect the curriculum of the students' lives. The learning is not just grounded in the prepared syllabus, the established, prescribed curriculum. *Problem posing* opens the door to ask questions and seek answers, not only of the visible curriculum, but also of the hidden curriculum. *Problem posing* is very interested in the hidden curriculum, which is why many are uncomfortable with it. *Problem posing* causes people to ask questions many do not want to hear. For example, in the following description of a family meeting, there is problem solving, which brings about a *feel-good* sensation, and there is problem posing, which causes some to feel uncomfortable. Both problem solving and problem posing are existing simultaneously with very different consequences. This family meeting took place in the school of Rainey and Carmen, whom you have previously met.

The problem to be solved was that parents had quit coming to the family meetings. Families felt alienated; teachers blamed them for not attending, and the state agency was asking why families weren't involved in the education of their children. The problem for the district was to get the families involved. They needed to solve this problem, or state funds would be cut. The school had a new principal who actively worked with Carmen, Rainey, and all the teachers to find ways to make the families feel more welcome and more involved. At this point, only Carmen was making visits to the students' homes. Soon, the principal started making visits with Carmen; eventually, she felt confident enough with her limited Spanish to make the visits alone. The families, of course, responded very positively. Other teachers began to visit the homes instead of sending messages home telling the parents to come to school. Soon, the teachers felt there was reason to believe that they could have a family meeting, and the families would come. The first meeting was scheduled. Invitations were sent to the families in their language; a door prize was offered; and the children were prepared to share during part of the meeting, which was scheduled to be held in the school auditorium.

The parents arrived and sat in the back rows. The teachers arrived and sat in the front row. Three empty rows of auditorium seats separated the parents and the teachers. The parents were welcomed by one of the teachers, and the children performed. A guest speaker from the state agency spoke to the families about the importance of their involvement in the education of their children.

Her presentation to the parents was articulate and forceful. She encouraged the parents to turn off the TV and talk with their children. She explained to the parents that what they teach at home is as valuable as what is taught in school. She followed this by talking about the transferal nature of language: What the kids know in Spanish, they will know in English, too. I could see the parents nodding their heads in agreement. She encouraged the parents to ask questions, and not just who, what, and where, but also, why.

The meeting lasted a little more than an hour. When it was over, the parents began to gather their tired children. Among the teachers in the first row there was general agreement that the meeting had been a success. They had solved their problem. The families came.

Why did I seem to be the only one who was disappointed? Very little meaningful interaction took place between the parents and the teachers. No one had asked the parents how they felt, what they needed, what their concerns were. The entire evening had been a monologue; the families had been talked at. I had hoped for a dialogue.

However, not all problems are so easily solved. Sometimes, problem posing spins off of problem solving. As the teachers were smiling among themselves, and the parents were beginning to gather their children, an older man, who looked more like a grandpa, stood up and faced the stage of the auditorium. Very seriously and respectfully, he addressed all of those in the front of the auditorium:

> "¿Por qué enseña a los niños en una lengua que no entienden y entonces los retienen?" he asked.
> (Why do you teach our children in a language that they don't understand and then flunk them?)

Silence hung in the room. No one answered him. Everyone silently left the auditorium. This is problem posing, as opposed to problem solving. The man had questioned the established processes, which were obviously failing. The children were not learning, and the state agency wanted to know why.

So did this man. This was a real problem, based on his lived experiences, which mattered to his family. He posed the problem, and many in the room came to understand that it is easier to problem solve than to problem pose.

TO GROOM

It all seemed so simple when all I had to worry about was teaching that *to groom* was an infinitive. Critical pedagogy enables us to think about what it means in the real world. For example, I was groomed to be a teacher, a secretary, or a nurse. No one ever specifically said that to me, but I received the message in multiple ways; I read my world. Very early I understood that I just didn't want to be a secretary or a nurse, so that left just one choice. I really never questioned it. As I reflect on those who groomed me, I am sure they were not aware of it, or they were doing what they thought was right for the time. My brother was never groomed to be a teacher, a secretary, or a nurse.

Grooming is preparing one group for a high-status place in life. *Grooming* is akin to putting one group on a superhighway and the other group on a rough and bumpy road. When the group on the highway arrives first, they assume that they got there because they deserved to, because they worked harder, because they are smarter. For my age group, it is particularly easy to understand grooming when we consider our own experiences. Little boys were groomed to be bosses; little girls were groomed to be secretaries. I think, as a society, we have developed more complex understandings of this process.

I literally had just written that sentence when an outraged Dawn, our daughter, called and read this article to me.

> Despite three decades of affirmative action, "glass ceilings" still block women and minority groups from the top management ranks of American industry, a bipartisan federal commission said Wednesday in the government's first comprehensive study of barriers to promotion.
>
> White men, while constituting about 43 percent of the work force, hold about 95 of every 100 senior management positions, defined as vice president and above, the report said.
>
> The Glass Ceiling Commission, which spent three years studying the issues, noted that 97 percent of senior managers in Fortune 1000 industrial corporations are white males, and only 5 percent of the top managers at Fortune 2000 industrial and service companies are women, virtually all of them white. Two thirds of the overall population and 57 percent of the work force are female or minority, or both. ("Glass ceiling intact," 1995)

I guess I was wrong about our developing more complex understandings about boys being groomed to be bosses and girls being groomed to be assistants. What a waste of talent; what a waste of resources when only a small part of the population is allowed into positions of authority. I do not believe that 95 to 97 percent of the men are smarter and more productive; I do believe that they were groomed for these positions by hidden institutional and societal processes that we have failed to recognize.

Grooming still exists in overt and covert ways. Race, class, and gender are variables that determine your path: the superhighway or the dirt road. Those of us who have bumped into the "glass ceiling" have a moral mandate not to let others behind us have the same experience. Have you ever visited Washington, DC? It is frightening to see the grooming of white people to rule and the grooming of brown people to serve. It is a tragic contradiction of life that, in the assumed center of democracy, it is so easy to see which race has been placed on the superhighway and which race has been placed on the bumpy, dirt road.

Sometimes, these processes of grooming are an inherent part of specific lesson designs. For example, in the following activity, who is being groomed?

Around the World

This is a great name for a not-so-great math activity. The overt objective is for students to have an opportunity to practice a skill or to memorize a fact. The objective in this particular class was to review addition by using flash cards. The real objective was to win. This is what happened on the day that I watched this activity.

Rainey, the teacher, sat on a chair in front of the room; the children were seated at four groups of tables. Two children stood up, and Rainey held up a flash card with an addition problem. The child who said the correct answer first, as determined by Rainey, was the winner. Then that child would move on to compete with the next child. The loser sat down. I studied the individual faces as they won and lost, stood up and sat down. The winners received cheers and applause from their peers and moved on for more practice. The losers sat down and did not get to practice. Thus, the ones who needed less, received more, and the ones who needed more, received less.

Despite my apprehension about this, the activity appeared to be a resounding success. All the children were squealing with glee. The principal passed the door and looked in with an approving look on his face. The lesson certainly appeared to be student centered and very interactive, not to mention fun! However, the primary focus of the activity was on the winning, not learning. Several students in particular caught my eye.

First, I noticed Irma, the cheerleader, who was a consistent loser. Each time someone said the numbers faster than she did, she had to sit down. She must be an amazingly resilient child because, each time after she sat down with a very dejected look on her face, she would quietly stare at the floor for about two minutes and then begin cheering wildly for the others again. I still do not know if Irma can add, but I'm not sure that it mattered in this activity.

The second child who caught my eye was Rosio, the loser who can add. Now, how could this happen? At the beginning of the game, I did not know Rosio, her math abilities, or her level of fluency in English. But I did notice that throughout the game, she was very quiet and still. When it came her turn to stand, she did so slowly and always was immediately forced to sit down because she didn't say anything. It appeared she could not add, but later I learned that she could add very well.

When the math activity ended, I asked Rainey if I could take Rosio to a little table and work with her. We began in Spanish, and Rosio communicated very little with me. I asked if she knew English, and she said yes. I asked her if she wanted me to use English or Spanish; she immediately replied, "English." Rosio answered 80 percent of the addition problems correctly. When she had trouble, she would count the beans we had on the table, and then she had 100 percent accuracy. Why, then, didn't she win some of the rounds of competition? Rosio is a very quiet and shy girl. She thinks carefully before answering.

This activity was designed to reward those who think and speak quickly and loudly; it also grooms those who know and eliminates those who need to know (Wink, 1991). Despite its great name, this activity benefits those who least need it. Those with the most, get the most. Those who need this type of structured practice stay in their seats. Sometimes these classroom activities are even more subtle, but just as deadly, because you have to be able to cut through sentimentality to understand the dynamics of power that are being constructed for one person or one group.

TO NAME

To name is to call an *ism* an *ism*: racism, classism, sexism. Naming is talking about the corruptible colonization, the damnable domination, the insidious supremacy that many marginalized groups have experienced but have been conditioned not to mention. The A Team gets huffy when they hear the B Team *name*. The A Team responds with sentences that begin, "Yeahbut, ..." *Naming* is talking honestly and openly about one's experiences with power and without power. For example, in the introduction to this edition, I named it: sexism.

Naming is more than just articulating a thought; it is more than just talking and labeling. *Naming* is when we articulate a thought that traditionally has not been discussed by the minority group nor the majority group. *Naming* takes place when the nondominant group tells the dominant group exactly what the nondominant group thinks and feels about specific social practices. *To name* is to take apart the complex relationships of "more" and "less" between the two groups. For example, when little girls tell little boys (or when women tell men) that they hate the "glass ceiling," they are naming. When women say they hate it that men, 43 percent of the workforce, hold 95 percent of the senior managerial positions ("Glass Ceiling Intact," 1995), they are naming. When ethnic minorities say that they hate it that the remaining 5 percent of those managers are women, and only white women, they are naming. When African Americans say they hate it when blacks in the public-sector jobs earn 83.3 percent of the median income of whites (Bancroft, 1995), they are naming.

A friend, Verena, who lives in one of the northern states, wrote me a long letter about a school at which she had found a job. She had discovered terrible racist policies that were hurting the group of Native Americans and African Americans. As she desperately needed this job, she was upset about what to do. She wrote, "I have to make a choice to teach and play the game, or expose what is going on. If I do that, I am sure that I will eventually lose my job." If Verena decides to expose the racist policies, she will be "naming." And, if she doesn't, it will be because she has a fear of naming.

When I went to college, I pretended that I couldn't type although I was very good. I didn't want to end up typing (as a secretary) for a man (as a boss). At that time I didn't have the language to articulate and name the gender-specific role that I could easily see might be assigned. Even if I would have had the thought and the language to be able to talk about why women shouldn't type for bosses, I would never have done it. Even if I could have named, I would have been afraid to name. I still struggle with this, but I am improving. Courage and patience.

TO MARGINALIZE

To *marginalize* is to place someone or something on the fringes, on the margins of power. To be marginalized is to be made to feel less. Sometimes teachers marginalize specific groups of students. Remember when I told you about my colleague who labeled some students *normal* and *regular*? That is marginalizing. What group has been devalued in the following phone conversation?

> TEACHER #1: Hi. This is Amy Jones. I understand that you are going to be my substitute tomorrow. I didn't leave any special plans. I want to tell you a little about my class and what you'll be doing tomorrow.
>
> TEACHER #2: Great! I'm glad you called.
>
> TEACHER #1: My room is way in the back of the school, Room 42. It's a sheltered English class. They are third, fourth, and fifth graders. Several languages are represented in this group.
>
> TEACHER #2:: Oh, I remember your class. I substituted in Room 43 yesterday, which is the special education class. I brought one of the students to your room so he could paint with your class. You may remember me.
>
> TEACHER #1: Sure, I remember you. But listen, my kids are great. They are normal. They aren't stupid or crazy like *those* kids next door.

Certain trigger words often give you a hint that marginalizing is coming, such as *normal*, *regular*, *those people*, and *them*. When you hear these, you can almost be assured that someone is going to be marginalized.

In the following statement that a teacher made to me during a staff development day, can you see which group has been marginalized?

> TEACHER A: Give me one of those Asians with glasses any day before a Mexican!

TO SCHOOL

Schooling refers to the hidden educational processes by which schools impose the dominant ways of knowing on all. We have been schooled to think in traditional ways. One problem with that is that we now often have schools filled with traditional teachers and nontraditional students.

For example, I have mentioned to you that I was schooled to write in a traditional way; it was linear, dense, distant, neutral, and boring—none of which I am. I wrote in academicese; I hid behind my jargon. As I reflect on my old writing, I can see more and more of my male professors in every sentence. My old writing reflects them very well. My writing of today reflects me. It is everything I was schooled not to do: tell stories, be circular, be passionate, use real language. More than anything else, I was schooled to believe that I was writing for someone else; it had never entered my head to write for me, to write to make sense of my thoughts.

I must not be the only one who had this experience. My grad students initially think they are writing for a grade in the grade book; they want to know exactly what I want; they want to know how many pages. I just want them to write and make meaning of ideas that are bouncing around in their heads. I want them to write and to get smarter. I will respond as I come along for the cognitive ride. Who knows what we will learn, but we will learn. Recently, I was reading Sandy's journal. Sandy is a young grandmother who is back in college.

I have been *schooled* to believe that my thoughts did not matter. For example, I have been *schooled* to believe that I should not share a thought unless I could cite the authority. I am learning now that my thoughts matter. This is so new that it can be scary. Being asked to think for myself and then commit it to paper is a challenge: It flies in the face of everything I have ever been conditioned to do. Schooling is alive and well in me (see Note 6).

TO SILENCE

I am still silenced a lot. I struggle with silence. Men can silence me more than any other group. The old socialized patterns run so deeply that it is hard for me to break them even when I understand and can articulate the dynamic. When committee meetings get "hot and heavy," I still sink into silence. Breaking the old domesticated patterns of silence is still a struggle for me. However, now I *see* silencing. Previously, when I was silenced, I did not know it; I did not understand it; I did not recognize it. If fact, I bought into it and supported it with my behaviors. When I was silenced, I cooperated and perpetuated the process. Now, when I am silenced, I understand what is happening. Now, I can name it. However, I still struggle with my fear of naming. Sometimes, when I am in university committee meetings with many full professors, I am painfully aware that the insidious dynamic of silencing is controlling the agenda; I am painfully aware of my own fear of naming. The invisible agenda of who speaks and who listens often takes my mind from the visible agenda. I am always aware of the delicate balance between courage and patience as we move critically together toward a more democratic society. In my own context, I have noticed that (a) most full professors are men; (b) some are aware that they are silencing others, and others are not aware; (c) the few full professors who are women do not silence me. I know that this tells much about my sociocultural context and about me. (I told you early in this book that I don't always like learning; this is one example.) However, my experiences have taught me that this social dynamic of silencing plays out every day in all contexts. Sometimes we just don't see it. I guess my message is that we should *see silencing* and *stop silencing*.

I watch in amazement in my grad classes when certain students speak freely, but I am particularly aware of those who are still silenced. They feel as deeply; they know as much. I watch which individuals are silenced by others. I watch which groups are silenced by other groups and have noticed that silencing has a certain pattern:

Often,

those who have more, silence those who have less;

those who are from the dominant European American culture silence those from non–European American cultures;

boys silence girls;

men silence women.

Often,

men don't know it;

boys don't know it;

European Americans don't know it, and

those with more don't know it.

Silencing is usually a quiet and insidious process. Sometimes those who are being silenced know it, and sometimes they don't. Those who are doing the silencing rarely know it.

Remember when I told you in the introduction to this edition that there were two pages in the first edition that triggered the most reactions? This is one of those pages. I simply could not tell you the number of people who have challenged this page, and I simply could not tell you the number of people who have said, "They do too know it." Multiple perspectives; the voice of "the other"; naming; power: These are all inherent in the concept of silencing. I think that is why it triggers such simultaneous and contradictory reactions. The second page in the book that always triggers a reaction is the metaphor of an A Team and a B Team.

TO SOCIALIZE

Society sends many messages to each of us. Sometimes we hear those messages, and sometimes we don't. However, when we consciously or unconsciously accept those messages and live those messages, we are being socialized.

This took place in a fourth-grade classroom when the teacher announced the students would clean out their desks on Friday. Throughout the week, the students waited patiently for the Great Cleaning Day. When Friday finally came, papers and books and giggles filled the room, except for one boy, who did not take part. This boy comes from a culture that believes little boys do not clean; little girls and women clean. His mother came after school to clean his desk as this was work not befitting a young man.

This example is quite vivid and easy to see. Many times we do not recognize, see, or understand the hidden socializing that is taking place. For example, from the point of view of this little boy and his mom, he is not being socialized; it is just the way things are. From the point of view of the teacher who told the story, it was an outrage. It is not really so different from the way I was socialized as a child. I cleaned; my brother did not.

Another example of socializing happened to us when we had an exchange student from Mexico. Laura was from Mexico City and came from a very enriched background that included ideas, books, laughter, love, and lots of money. Her family had many servants to make life easier. She left the urban confines of Mexico City and came to the desert ranch to live with us.

Suddenly, we realized that she had never done any of the indoor or outdoor chores that we had socialized Dawn and Bo to believe were part of everyone's responsibility. Washing and ironing clothes presented a particularly sensitive area. Bo and Dawn were in junior high and high school, respectively, and had been doing this for themselves for years. Dawn, as a grade-school feminist, was quick to make sure that if she did her own clothes, her little brother sure would do his. Bo grew up believing that if I washed his treasured T-shirts (a.k.a. rags) and jeans, they would be ruined with hot water or a hot drier. I socialized him to believe that only *he* could take care of *his* clothes. Now, suddenly both of our kids were very eager to see if I would wash and iron *Laura's* clothes. They understood my vulnerable position as it related to justice, equity, and culture, and they relished every minute of my dilemma. After reflection, I realized that I couldn't undo all of my socializing of my own kids and that Laura would have to learn to wash and iron her own clothes. I can still remember all three of the kids standing in the washroom while Bo and Dawn smugly taught Laura how to wash. Laura did all of her own washing; she never did iron, but then neither did Dawn and Bo. Laura is back in Mexico City now and no longer washes her own clothes. She is now socializing others to believe it is their job.

VOICE

Walk into any classroom, any teachers' lounge, any school office and see if you can tell who has voice. Who uses *voice* to express their perspective?

Their viewpoint? Their way of knowing? Whose voice is promoted and valued? Whose voice is discredited with a wave of the hand? Courage is related to voice; it takes courage for some to express their voice. *Voice* is the use of language to paint a picture of one's reality, one's experiences, one's world. I am more interested in the voice that traditionally has not been heard.

The voice of those who traditionally have not been heard is usually embedded with varying degrees of resistance, rage, and a hint of resolve. I vividly recall, as a little girl, standing in a rural, isolated spot where the gas station/general store was the hub of the community for many, many miles. I remember the two outhouses behind the store: One had an old sign that said "Whites Only" and the other had an old sign that said "Indians." I remember looking at the signs and knowing something was terribly wrong, but I said nothing. I had no voice. I remember being asked to carry moldy bread onto the Sioux Indian reservation to the various families. I can still feel the shame I felt handing the bread to the women who answered their doors. But I would never have dreamed of expressing myself. I had no voice. My resistance, rage, and resolve were silenced. Most of my life has been dominated by the voice of one powerful group. This *monovoice* has been very limiting for many. As we near the end of the century, more and more voices are being heard. Multiple voices are moving us forward. The broader the diversity of voices, the greater the quality of society. Our society is becoming more vibrant, more enriched, and more exciting. It represents more of us. This traditional *monovoice* is transforming itself into a new *multivoice*, and not everyone is happy about it.

The following voice comes from Sheila, who is discovering hers as she prepares to be a teacher.

> *I wonder how much voice I will have when I'm teaching. I have recently left a career in management to become a teacher. During my years in management, I became one of the top employees where I worked: top in responsibility, not in authority. It seemed to me that the "voices" of women were not valued because the system was "just fine."*
>
> *The majority of teachers are women, but their voices are just whispers. Women and minorities need to be at the top levels of school systems, and we need more men at the elementary teaching level.*
>
> *Cummins (1989) said, "Unless we ourselves are empowered, we cannot be involved with any other processes of empowerment. To be voiceless is to be powerless. If we view ourselves as helpless, we are." I thought that it must be easy for him to say. He is a man, not a woman teaching in the elementary school with others holding her future in their hands.*

As Sheila is discovering her voice, she is *voicing* one of the most difficult questions of the study of critical pedagogy: Why so few women? Why
so many men? Critical pedagogy has caused me to reflect seriously on the
moral mandate that falls to those of us (women and minorities) who have
survived a career of trying to change the system. My experience teaches me
that many women see and know in critical ways and are moving to voice. I
note with interest that we are in good company when we move into relearning and unlearning. In a dialogue, Donaldo Macedo is asking Paulo Freire
how he would respond to his omission of the voice of women in his earlier
works. Freire responds by saying, "I believe that the question feminists in
the United States raise concerning my treatment of gender in *Pedagogy of
the Oppressed* is not only valid but very timely" (Macedo, 1994, p. 106).

The purpose of this chapter has been to focus on one central question:
What in the world is critical pedagogy? My intention has been for you to discover meaning based on your own experiences and knowledges. My purpose has not been to provide a list of definitions for you. However, on the
very day on which I was finishing this chapter, I found a piece of paper
among a large stack of graduate students' work on my desk; it was entitled
Scribble Notes. The first paragraph seemed like a powerful definition of critical pedagogy for those who would like to have it. As I say, sometimes these
definitions just fall from heaven. Lily, a teacher, wrote:

Critical pedagogy is a process of learning and relearning. It entails a
sometimes painful reexamination of old practices and established
beliefs of educational institutions and behaviors. Critical pedagogy
causes one to make inquiries about equality and justice. Sometimes
these inequalities are subtle and covert. The process requires
courage and patience. Courage promotes change and democracy
provides all learners equal access to power.

What in the world is critical pedagogy? It is certainly more than is written in this chapter, and it is as much as we allow it to be in our own ways, in
our own communities. Critical pedagogy is more than the sum of its parts; it
is more than a list of definitions of the words that have come to be associ-
ated with it. Lily, wisely, did not fall into the trap of seeing only the separate
words of critical pedagogy. She put it together holistically after much reading and reflection. She made meaning of all the parts based on her experiences in life and in schools. Critical pedagogy is a process that enables
teachers and learners to join together in asking fundamental questions about
knowledge, justice, and equity in their own classroom, school, family, and
community.

> *Beatriz visited a designated bilingual classroom in the school where she teaches. As she entered, she noticed the room was physically divided by the strategic placement of the desks, which divided the room in half. The English-speaking students were on one side of the room, and the Spanish-speaking students were on the opposite side. When the students began reading, the Spanish-dominant students read in a Spanish basal with the aide. The teacher worked only with the English-dominant students and chose themes from the core literature, which was in English. The thematic unit and core literature were totally unrelated to what the Spanish-dominant children were reading.*

Beatriz told us that before her study of critical pedagogy, she would have thought this was a good bilingual classroom because the Spanish-dominant children were using their primary language. However, now she understands the perpetuated inequity, which is done, in this particular instance, under the guise of bilingual education in this classroom. Critical pedagogy is a lens that empowers us to see and to know in new ways. When we last spoke with Beatriz, she had begun a dialogue with her colleague in this classroom. Critical pedagogy leads us from silence to voice.

In this chapter, the language of critical pedagogy has been seen in real classroom experiences with the hope that it will help readers to generate and expand their own meanings for critical pedagogy. In the next chapter, I will examine the question: Where in the world did it come from? Before moving on, are there other words and ideas of critical pedagogy that are meaningful for you? Language is never static; it continues to grow and change.

LOOKING AHEAD FOR YOUR THOUGHTS AND LANGUAGE ON CRITICAL PEDAGOGY

What are your own words and ideas?

NOTES

1. For definitions of the language of critical pedagogy, I refer to the books surrounding my computer chair at this very moment: (a) several by McLaren; any of his three editions of *Life in Schools: An Introduction to Critical Pedagogy in the Foundations of Education*; (b) Giroux (1988); (c) Harris and Hodges (1995); (d) Kanpol (1994); and (e) Leistyna, Woodrum, & Sherblom (1996). The truth is that there are marvelous definitions in these various books. I love some of them. I strongly encourage you to reflect on others' definitions. As you do, you will notice that each definition of critical pedagogy varies with each person and each page and each book. How could it not? Experience is inherent within critical pedagogy. These books and others to which I refer throughout this text will provide definitions that move you to other levels of complexities of understandings. Remember, one of my not-so-hidden goals in this book is to lead you to other books. Perhaps, you might like to start with the glossary in the back of deMarrais & LeCompte (1999).

2. Gee (1992; 1996) provides very thorough and meaningful perspectives on discourse in these two books. His image of discourse as an identity kit is helpful for many who are struggling with this concept. In addition, he weaves tight connections between discourses and literacies. In fact, I would suggest you read Gee and McQuillan at the same time; they're guaranteed to make you think more critically about literacy.

3. Critical literacies. If you are intrigued with this concept, I strongly recommend that you read *Critical literacy: Politics, Praxis, and the Postmodern* (1993) by Colin Lankshear and Peter McLaren, published by SUNY at Albany, New York; *Literacies of Power* (1994) by Donaldo Macedo, Westview Press, Boulder, Colorado; *Literacy: Reading the Word and the World* (1987) by Paulo Freire and Donaldo Macedo, published by Bergin and Garvey of South Hadley, Massachusetts; and *With Literacy and Justice for All: Rethinking the Social in Language and Education* (1991) by Carole Edelsky, published by Falmer Press of Bristol, Pennsylvania. The topic of critical literacies is just too deep and too wide for the confines of this little book.

4. An example of this is Jeff McQuillan (1998) in which he uses his own critical literacy to deconstruct the popular notion of a literacy crisis. In addition, he demonstrates how this notion makes it easier for us to ignore the serious pedagogical hurdles that students face in their literacy development. This book may very well be an unlearning experience for some readers. Remember, this is good.

5. Cummins (1996) says human relationships are at the heart of school (p. 1). He then expands the concept to demonstrate how these relation-

ships, which we teachers establish, have the power to open the door for students to grow and develop freely or to wither and fade painfully.

6. Parker Palmer (1998, p. 18) tells a wonderful anecdote about assigning an autobiographical essay. One student asked if it would be okay to use "I" or would that knock off half a grade. In fact, Parker never mentions critical pedagogy, but his ideas extend this discussion to a broader context of humanness, justice, equity, and morality grounded in critical pedagogy. Through his book, I was led to Florida Scott-Maxwell (1983, p. 42), who, when she was in her 80s, said, "You need only claim the events of your life to make yourself yours. When you truly possess all you have been and done . . . you are fierce with reality." Experience, reflection, honesty, action: This is all a part of critical pedagogy, even, if the word is never used.

chapter 3

Critical Pedagogy
Where in the World Did It Come From?

Throughout this text, I hope to make critical pedagogy more meaningful for teachers and learners by sharing four central questions about critical pedagogy: What is it? Where did it come from? How do we do it? And, why does it matter? The spirit of inquiry that is fundamental to critical pedagogy has caused me to seek answers for these questions. In the previous chapter, I wrote about the big ideas in critical pedagogy: What in the world is it? In this chapter, we will follow the roots of critical pedagogy from the Latin Voice, to the European Voice, and finally to the multiple voices of North America. I realize that when I begin to speak of the critical voices of North America, I will inevitably omit someone. Therefore, in this chapter I will direct my comments to the critical theorists who have most directly influenced my own experiences and thinking during the last few years. My purpose is to tell the big story that lies behind those big words and ideas. The historical roots of critical pedagogy, as seen in Figure 3.1, spread to many parts of the world. As I paint this picture, I will ground it in the reality of teachers' voices.

THE LATIN VOICE

Freire: The Foundation

Let me introduce you to the Paulo Freire I love. I have a tiny tape recorder that often can be found on my windowsill above the kitchen sink. When I

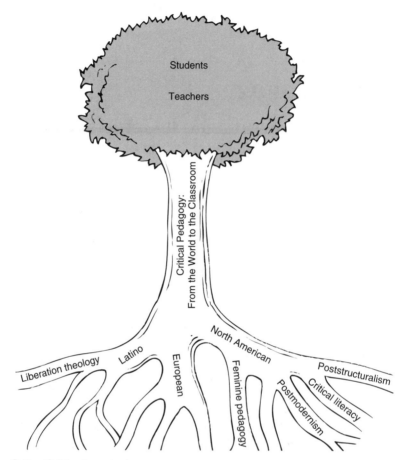

FIGURE 3.1 Critical roots

begin to lack courage, or when I need more patience, I play only one tape: Paulo Freire (1993).

This is a recording I made of him speaking to several thousands of people in southern California, but when I listen to this tape, I still feel as if he were speaking only to me. During this presentation, he spoke of two concepts: teaching and learning. As I listened, the seeds for this book were planted. As we were walking away, Dawn said, "Mom, he's just like Gandhi, only with clothes on."

For me, he is the quintessential teacher and learner. Freire has taught many things to many people all over the world. When I read his words, when I hear his words, I learn and relearn to focus on teaching and learning that is rigorous and joyful (Freire, 1994; Gadotti, 1994).

Much of multicultural critical pedagogy in North America today stands on the shoulders of this giant: Paulo Freire. He taught me the difference between "reading the word and the world." During the 1960s, Freire conducted a national literacy campaign in Brazil for which he eventually was jailed and exiled from his own country. He not only taught the peasants to read, he taught them to understand the reasons for their oppressed condition. The sounds, letters, and words from the world of his adult learners were integrated and codified. Ideas, words, and feelings joined together to generate a powerful literacy that was based on the learners' lived experiences. The Brazilian peasants learned to read the words rapidly because they had already read the world, and their world was the foundation for reading the words. Traditionally, literacy has been the process of reading only the word. Emancipatory literacy is reading the world. Freire was not jailed and exiled because he taught peasants to "read the word," but because he taught the subordinate class to critically read the world (Freire & Macedo, 1987). Freire taught the peasants to use their knowledge and their literacy to examine and reexamine the surrounding power structures of the dominant society.

Freire teaches that no education is politically neutral. Traditionally, teachers (that would include me) have assumed that we don't have to bother with politics; teaching is our concern. I see on my resume that one of the first state conference presentations I ever gave was entitled "Teaching, I Love. It's the Politics I Hate." I now think that I was pretty naive, and maybe even elitist, to think that teaching and learning could possibly take place in a vacuum. Every time we choose curriculum, we are making a political decision. What will I teach, and what won't I teach? The social, cultural, and political implications are great. After reading Freire, a local teacher sent me this E-mail.

Freire left me with a new insight. I had never thought about the role of passivity. Before, I did not look at passivity as being active. This oxymoron is new to me. I am learning that these contradictions are confounding and enlightening.

Schools are social; they are filled with real people who live in real communities and have real concerns. People with multiple perspectives send their kids to schools. Teaching and learning are a part of real life, and real life includes politics and people. Schools do not exist on some elevated pure plain of pedagogy away from the political perspectives of people. If two friends sit down for a social visit, politics is a part of it. If hundreds of kids from a neighborhood come to school, politics is a part of it. Paulo Freire recognized this before many others in education. If educators state that they are neutral, then they are on the side of the dominant culture. "Passivity is also a powerful political act," a student said to me. Teaching is learning.

Traditionally, the *strong* voice of school has been very homogeneous along the lines of race, class, and gender. Historically, the *strong* have been the A Team, and the *weak* have been the B Team. The *weak* have been underrepresented and not heard. This is changing, and change is hard. Twenty-five years ago I wrote in a private journal that I thought we would go "kicking and screaming" into a multicultural society at the turn of the century. I remember feeling rather neutral, distant, and clever when I wrote it. I had no idea how difficult it would be for us as a society to change. Change makes the *strong* feel weakened, and the *weak* feel strengthened.

I recognize that words like A Team, B Team, strong, and weak can be very jarring and disquieting. I also realize that sometimes that is what it takes to trigger critical self-reflection. At least for me. I have not always been known to immediately welcome and embrace new ideas, new challenges, and new perspectives. Sometimes, words and experiences had to disturb me to my deepest core before I could think new thoughts and take new actions. Power is never conceded easily; things shake, rattle, and roll first. I suspect that this is true for a great many of us.

Demographically, the world has changed, and nowhere are those changes experienced more profoundly than in classrooms today. Many classes are filled with traditional teachers and nontraditional students, conventional teachers and nonconventional students. The past is past; it is not necessarily bad, but it is past. We all must move forward. We cannot continue to use old answers for new questions. The questions have changed, and together we are seeking new answers for new questions. Critical pedagogy has helped me rethink old questions, and Paulo Freire has helped me search for new answers.

This year I had an experience in the Minneapolis airport that demonstrated to me how much change has taken place. I had three hours to wait, and I spent the time walking, looking, and trying to enjoy myself. I was very aware of a most uncomfortable feeling; I felt out-of-sync, a vague feeling of apprehension and uneasiness. As I became more and more aware of my feelings, I tried to analyze why I was feeling that way. After a couple of hours of strolling and musing, it hit me: Everyone looked just like me; it was like a world full of Joan clones. One generation ago, a homogeneous world was the only world I knew. It made me reflect on how much had actually changed, and how we change with the changes. It's moments like these that give me hope.

Labeling Freire. Paulo Freire has been labeled "the most labeled educator." He has been labeled Marxist, idealistic, liberal, national-developmentalist, new schoolist, inductivist, spontaneist, nondirectivist, and Catholic neo-anarchist (Gadotti, 1994, p. 126). My spell-check has trouble with some of these labels; I do, too. I have heard him called a communist, a revolutionary, a philosopher, and a genius. Lots of labels. He has been called the authentic intellectual in our world, an ancient sage, and in his own words, humble warrior of the spirit (Gadotti, 1994). Of all the labels for Paulo Freire that I have heard, the one I love the best is the one my spell-check uses: *Freer*. Yes!

Since the publication of the first edition, Paulo Freire has died. If Paulo were alive today, these are the three things I would like to tell him. Why would I tell him these things? I would do it because I know he would respond in a way that would give me courage and patience.

> First, it's a tough time to be a bilingual teacher educator; it's a great time to be bilingual. Dickens was right: These are the best of times; these are the worst of times. When we ask people if they are for bilingual education, most will say no. When we ask people if they want their kids to be bilingual, most will say yes. As any parent knows (or as any researcher knows), how you ask the question determines the answer you get (see Note 1).

> Second, I would tell him that this is how I felt when I sat down last fall to make my bilingual reading/language arts syllabus to reflect state mandates.

Out With Freire: In With Phonemes.   Out with meaning; in with minutiae. Out with schema; in with the schwa; out with the whole, in with the parts. With the state guidelines dictating that I must prepare credential students with a knowledge of fricatives, phonemes, and phonology, the truth is that I find myself feeling philosophically frustrated. This would be funny, if it weren't fact.

> Third, I would tell Paulo that for much of the semester I placed the emphasis on the relationship between sound and letter. We did phonemic awareness activities in English and in Spanish. We took quizzes on phonemics, phonology, and phonetics. I'll take that group of students and match their knowledge on the new, state-mandated, sound-centric test of how-to-teach-reading with any other group in the state. The students knew the information when I gave the tests. Do they know it today? I doubt it.

Now, here is the point of all of this: At the end of the semester, it was clear what they had learned, and it was equally clear what they hadn't learned. I shudder with chagrin.

So what will I do the next time I teach reading/language arts to the bilingual credential students?

Here is my plan: I will read like crazy and make sure they see me reading. I will share all of my reading and writing with them on a weekly basis. I will challenge their assumptions; I will invite them to share my struggles when my own assumptions are challenged. I will do all I can to validate their language and their culture and their innate thirst for knowledge. I will do what my knowledge and experience tells me is the best for me and for the students in my classroom.

Yes, I will teach the new test also. I will teach it on Friday nights, Saturdays, and Sundays. I will use direct instruction and drill. And, I will not charge them. When my students go to take that test, they will be as prepared as anyone.

Paulo, I will continue to go to every class armed with your legacy to me: rigor and joy; rigor and joy; rigor and joy. This is my pedagogy of hope, and I thank you.

Reflecting on Paulo Freire now reminds me of a story I heard Maxine Greene tell (April 17, 1998) about the last time she was with Paulo Freire before he died, as they were eating together in New York. Nita's (Paulo's widow) 10 year-old grandson was with them for the lunch and kept trying to jump into the conversation.

> *"We hotshots," Maxine said, "continued to talk and ignored the little boy's questions."*
>
> *The young boy continued to interrupt, and the adults continued to ignore his comments. Finally, Paulo halted the adult conversation and called attention to his young grandson:*
>
> *"Be quiet," Paulo said to the adults, "Every time you ignore a person's question, you dehumanize him."*

This statement struck me, and I hope I never forget it when I am teaching a class. I hope that I never forget it wherever I am.

Labels I Love to Hate.   Paulo Freire and Tove Skutnabb-Kangas were two of the first voices I read who made me stop and think about our use of labels in North American educational institutions. It was one of those hey-I-never-thought-of-that-experiences for me. For example, think of the word *minority*. From Freire (Freire & Macedo, 1987) I learned that it is often laden with connotations of less-less of something.

> Do you see how ideologically impregnated the term "minority" is? When you use "minority" in the U.S. context to refer to the majority of people who are not part of the dominant class, you alter its semantic value. When you refer to "minority" you are, in fact, talk-

ing about the "majority" who find themselves outside the sphere of political and economic dominance. In reality, as with many other words, the semantic alteration of the term "minority" serves to hide the many myths that are part of the mechanism sustaining cultural dominance. (pp. 124–125)

Recently, a teacher was complaining that her students "weren't intelligent" and "couldn't learn." However, she was particularly annoyed because "most are minorities." Wait. Most are minorities? Then, wouldn't they be majorities? Traditionally, I think we thought of the words *minority* and *majority* in a numerical sense. Minority meant less; majority meant more. Something has changed. If not numbers, then what in the world are we talking about? More and more, my sense is that when schools complain that they have so many "minorities," the hidden message is that the "minorities" have less value than the "majorities."

No one has been more personally involved with my own unlearning than Tove Skutnabb-Kangas. And, yes, not every minute of my own unlearning has been fun. It has happened again since the first edition. Skutnabb-Kangas demonstrates that when we (that includes me) in North America stop using the word *minority,* we deny students their legal protection under international agreements. She reminded us that when we use terms such as *linguistically diverse students* and other euphemisms, we actually rob students of the only protection they have in international human rights law (March 20, 1998). Linguistically diverse students have no protection in international law; minority students do (in press, 2000).

Ouch. Critical pedagogy teaches us to name, to reflect critically, to act. Tove named, I have reflected critically, and now I must act. In public, in policy-making, in publishing, I will use the word *minority*. However, my respect and love for Tove is superceded only by my complete disdain for the way I have heard the word *minority* used by some educators in North American schools to completely discredit the experiences, the cultures, and the languages of students (a) who have not yet acquired English, (b) come from cultures other than European ancestry, and (c) are often the numerical majority in the school. Therefore, I know I will continue my attempt to find language that describes students, if that information is necessary to add meaning to the context. For example, if they are bilingual and that information fits the context, I often say bilingual.

I didn't say this would be easy. My best rule-of-thumb is to find a meaningful adjective rather than a label (see Note 2).

Cummins (1996) writes in his preface of the same difficult issue. He generally tries to avoid the words *minority* and *majority* because of their pejorative connotations and inaccurate reflection of schools in the United States. However, he notes that in the European and Canadian contexts, the term *minority* is generally not laden with negative connotations; in fact, its very use guarantees certain legal and constitutional rights.

The legacy of Paulo Freire is pushing me to unlearn other labels. I know of a junior high school that proudly boasts of its Potentially At-risk Program. I can almost guarantee that all the kids placed in that program will end up "at risk." Labels can lead to tracks, which are an insidious form of social sorting. Sometimes we don't like to be bothered with this issue of labels. I think we need to bother ourselves more with the hidden implications of our language. What we say matters. The rationale of that's-the-way-we've-always-said-it just doesn't work for me any longer. However, sometimes the issue of labels and its devastating effects are exceedingly clear for almost everyone to understand. For example, a teacher told me she was visiting another classroom in her school. Within the first half hour of her visit, the teacher of that class had pointed out the "losers" in his room. Every student in the class heard his comments, and she noted that every one of the "losers" was either brown, black, or poor.

THE EUROPEAN VOICE

Critical pedagogy also has been influenced by voices from Europe. In the following sections, I will trace the roots of multicultural critical pedagogy in North American schools back to social and political contexts of other places and other times. The theory of reproduction, which started as an economic, political, and social idea, continues to thrive in schools today, but it is much more difficult to see and to understand than when it was a faraway idea in the history books. This part of the chapter will look at the early ideas of resistance that are alive and well in the critical pedagogy of today.

Gramsci

The word *hegemony*, the domination of one group over another, can be traced to the Italian social theorist Gramsci (see Note 3). He believed that hegemony was how societal institutions maintained their power, even by force if necessary. Gramsci (1971) also believed it was important for educators to recognize and acknowledge the existing oppressive structures inherent in schools. Power is a fundamental societal issue. As western industrial societies grow more sophisticated, power is less likely to be used in a physical manner and more likely to be used in subtle ways that are harder to see because even the dominated group is partially supporting the process. Hegemony takes place when the B Team smiles and keeps quiet because (a) it is the polite, appropriate way to behave; (b) they have been schooled to behave that way; and/or (c) it is safe. These hegemonic smiles take time and emotional energy. I know. When the dominated group behaves this way, the dominating group often thinks of them as "respectful." Counterhegemonic behaviors are filled with risk, insecurity, and not many smiles. They also take lots of time and emotional energy. I know.

Hegemony are 12- and 13-year-old girls who suddenly begin to do poorly in math and science courses. It is not that girls are less intelligent; it is that they are partially supporting the process of believing that boys know more about numbers and problem solving. Hegemony takes place when Spanish-dominant families support English-only processes. Hegemony takes place when one of the Hmong-American graduate students in our program comes into every class and sits towards the back of the room and remains silent throughout the class. Many of the majority students think he is the nicest, most "respectful" colleague. It is only during my office hours, when the door is closed, that I hear of his anger. He hopes he can move into counterhegemonic behaviors in his life time. But then what will his former colleagues think? He is beginning his doctoral program now, so I suspect I will learn.

Hegemony and counterhegemony are painful concepts. Critical pedagogy calls us to name. In my pre–critical pedagogy days when I was a nice Spanish teacher, I avoided words like hegemony. I just lived it. Now, in my post–critical pedagogy time of life, I try not to be a part of hegemonic processes. I am sure I slip sometimes. And when I enter into counterhegemony, it is not easy, but it is honest and authentic based on my lived experiences. From Gramsci, I have learned that in subtle and insidious ways, we can all be a part of maintaining myths.

Marx

The economic and social ideas of Karl Marx form important roots of critical pedagogy. Marx believed education was being used as an insidious vehicle for institutionalizing elite values and for indoctrinating people into unconsciously maintaining these values.

Marxist thought challenges the way in which the dominant ideology is reproduced through the use of *myths* (Macedo, 1994), which offer a sound bite to legitimize processes of oppression. One is the prevailing myth of a classless America: we're-all-alike-and-all-have-equal-access-to-opportunity-in-this-great-land. I have noticed that people who believe this tend not to hob-nob with the folks who know it isn't true. Myths are used as tools so the have-nots will affirm and support the processes that benefit the haves. A glaring example is the way George Bush in 1988 campaigned on the notion of a classless America while at the same time fighting for a capital gains tax to benefit the rich and threatening to veto a tax cut for the middle class (Macedo, 1994). The gulf between the social groups continues to widen, although some would have us think the gulf is not there.

Marx's ideas of reproduction are reflected in every classroom with subtle and hidden processes in which social classes are classified and grouped. Schools call it tracking. Sometimes, social classes suddenly are acknowledged, even by those who have traditionally denied them. They are publicly identified if they can be used to legitimize processes that hurt other groups of kids. For example, during an inservice teacher education workshop, a group of teachers was discussing what they could do to serve more effectively the needs of bilingual kids. The principal of this school, who had been a very reluctant participant throughout the inservice, could stand it no longer and suddenly made an announcement in a loud voice to the group:

"Oh, we don't have any LEPs in our school. The problem we have is poor white trash."

The teachers passively hung their heads—I think with shame—but they did not challenge her. My hunch is that the "poor white trash" in this school will be tracked for as long as they can stand to stay in school.

Labeling Marx. Whereas Freire had many labels, I think it would be safe to label Marx a Marxist. So the question becomes, What is a Marxist? What does it feel like to be in a Marxist classroom? I recently had the opportunity to ask these questions of students in a writing composition class.

What does a Marxist, the teacher, in this classroom look like? A lot like several hundreds of other teachers whom I have known. He was sitting in a circle with 25 students who had lots of books on their desks and appeared (to me) to be eager to learn, which I later found to be true. The teacher explained to me that the class was not studying Marx; rather, they were simply teaching and learning with a Marxist approach. My original question began to change a little: What is a Marxist approach to pedagogy? The students jumped right into the dialogue and told me.

A Marxist Approach to Pedagogy

It reignited my desire to learn.
It forces me to think.
Anyone can ask and answer questions.
We take time to learn.
It is applicable to my life.
It connects me to my imagination.
It always seeks other views.

The students discussed their frustration with other classes in which they had to write down everything the professor said and then return the same knowledge on a test. They spoke of their yearning to know of multiple paths to teaching and learning.

Freire and Marx provide deep roots for critical pedagogy that are reflected in learners turning their beliefs into behaviors for self and social transformation. The ideas we grapple with are not just for the safe confines of the four walls of the classroom. The whole idea is to improve the quality of life for ourselves and for others in our community. The mere momentum of the status quo will keep us in a vacuum unless we walk out the door and seek other ways of knowing.

These students in the composition class were actively engaged with new ideas; they were socially generating new knowledge; they were cogitating; and they were reading challenging books. This all seemed good to me. So I asked them: If this pedagogy is working so well, why is Marx the bad guy to so many North Americans?

"He messes up the control," one young man quietly said. His classmates nodded their heads in agreement.

I have noticed that when the subject of Marx comes up, a confrontation often follows. Confrontation is great sport for some, particularly those who have more control and power. Confrontation is more difficult for others, particularly those who have less control and power. Marx hands us a mirror and makes us look at our traditional patterns of control in schooling, patterns that run along the lines of race, class, and gender (see Note 4).

The Frankfurt School of Critical Theory

The Frankfurt School of Critical Theory of the 1940s believed schools were a vehicle for reproduction (a.k.a., tracked for life) whereby the workers who were needed in the existing power structures of society were prepared. These critical theorists postulated that the schools not only reproduce what skills society needs, but people with the corresponding social and personal demeanor as well. Gee (1990) updates this notion and shares his perspective:

> Schools have historically failed with nonelite populations and have thus replicated the social hierarchy, thereby advantaging the elites in the society. This has ensured that large numbers of lower socio-economic and minority people engage in the lowest level and least satisfying jobs in the society (or no jobs), while being in a position to make few serious political or economic demands on the elites.

Indeed, the fact that they have low literacy skills can be used (by themselves and the elites) as a rationale for them to be in low-level jobs and the elites in higher level ones. . . . (p. 31)

Sometimes, reproduction is easier to see than other times. Tracking is often one of the institutionalized processes that is very visible, but the reproduction of the status quo and the existing power structures are more invisible. In one district I know, they have the usual tracks: snob track, poor-white-trash track, Spanish/Portuguese track, and a new one that I just recently became aware of, the middle-class track. Remember, I do not make up these stories; these are words I repeatedly hear. The students who are tracked through these colored institutionalized processes reflect and reproduce themselves again and again.

TEACHER #1: Yes, it's yellow for the Asians, red for the Mexicans. It's the way they segregate the kids.

TEACHER #2: Yeah. That way if an Asian moves to another school, he'll be on the same track.

TEACHER #3: Yes, that's how they segregate at our school, too. Yellow for the Asians, red for the Mexican, and green for the white trash.

Tove Skutnabb-Kangas

Let me introduce you to Tove Skutnabb-Kangas, whom I know and love. She often brings out a strong response when people meet her, and the same was true for me. I had read her works for years, so I was prepared for the power of her thoughts, but I was not prepared for her personality. No one had ever told me.

Since the day I met her, the Easter Bunny and Malcolm X will forever be wedded in my mind. Let me explain. We were in a county school office presentation room; tables, chairs, and teachers filled the room. When I walked in, I noted a general air of excitement and happiness. I recognized the sound I heard: the happy hum of learning. Tove was moving among the teachers as they worked at tables; I could hear thoughtful questions and chuckles of joy throughout the room. I stood in the back of the room for about 10 minutes and simply enjoyed watching and experiencing the entire environment. "So, this is the famous Tove Skutnabb-Kangas," I thought.

Tove is of medium height and build; she has blonde curly hair that does exactly what it wants to do; and, she has round, round cheeks with the pinkest skin I have ever seen. Not white, but pink. The minute I met her, I thought of the round little nose and cheeks of the Easter Bunny. When she smiles, her face lights up the room. On that day, she was wearing brilliant colors with a long flowing skirt that had sequins sewn in so there was a kind of twinkle and reflection as she walked. She had on a fuchsia T-shirt, with a multicolored scarf and a darker jacket. For me, there is this aura of a cuddly Easter Bunny about Tove. A very powerful Easter Bunny, indeed.

She came to our campus and worked with teachers and learners in the area. While she was here, she met and visited with one of my male colleagues who had previously heard me describe her. When she left, he said, "Easter bunny, huh? Maybe a pink Malcolm X." Her ideas are strong, and her love is soft. When I see her, which is never often enough, I am filled with joy. We laugh and hug and hug and laugh. Then, we begin to discuss powerful ideas.

I have noticed that not everyone reacts to Tove the way I did during my initial encounter with her. In fact, sometimes the power of her ideas gives people a tummy ache. Sharon, a teacher/grad student, shares her story.

I first met Tove at a conference in San Francisco. I sat in the front row of the enormous auditorium. I didn't want to miss a word, an inference, a smile.

Soon, an official of the conference introduced Tove Skutnabb-Kangas, and I immediately noticed her rosy cheeks. Everyone applauded as Tove stepped up to the microphone and began talking loudly about education and language. Where was this soft cuddly bunny rabbit I had heard about? I was so confused. I sat up in my chair so I could try to grasp the words. What? I, as a teacher, was cutting off the native language of my bilingual students? Me, who is so dedicated? My preconceived notions exploded! Well, yes it is true, I only speak English, and I don't know the language of my students.

I sat up even straighter and thought seriously about leaving the room. How could I get out of here? My professor was sitting two seats away. This message was not comfortable for me to hear. I mean, how could I be hurting children?

I listened painfully and quickly left the room when Tove finished. I was enraged, hurt, confused, and angry. Later that week in class, we talked about the conference. My professor began talking about how wonderful it was to listen to Tove. All of a sudden she said, "Sharon, tell your colleagues about Tove." I could feel my face turning red, and I had to say, "Well, I really didn't care for her. I thought she was very loud and angry."

For the next year I read, reflected, mused, read, reflected, and mused before I came to terms with my feelings. Tove was not saying that I was a bad teacher, only that I was not meeting the academic needs of multilingual students in their primary language.

Yes, I could teach them in English, I could give them love and build their self-esteem. I could not, however, give them what they really needed to succeed in an English-speaking world: literacy and cognitive development. Even as I worked with the students on oral English development, they would start to fall behind their classmates cognitively and linguistically.

Now, you have met two Toves, or at least one very complex person. You will have to draw your own conclusions. Let me share with you a more formal introduction to Tove Skutnabb-Kangas, the internationally known Finnish linguist. She is a critical theorist with deep roots throughout many parts of Europe. She has worked throughout the world as a sociolinguistic and change agent. However, because of her numerous trips to the United States, many (like me) have come to know her almost as if she were a part of the North American voice. She has challenged many of us to think and rethink in critically relevant ways. She consistently asks us to look again at the processes by which the norm gets normalized.

In her writings and her presentations, she has raised the issue of linguistic genocide in our schools. Students enter our schools speaking languages from all over the world; 12 years later, they leave our school, speaking only English. Then we immediately want them to go to college and study *foreign* languages. Tove asks us to rethink this practice. And, she asks us to consider why it is taking place. Other countries often use direct and brutal tactics to prevent minority languages. In the United States our methods are indirect and more effective. When students are not served in their mother tongue, and when students are not allowed to use their own language to construct meaning, we are all part of the process that normalizes the majority use of English and disenfranchises all other languages. Or as Tove has repeatedly said, "We kill languages every day in our classes."

I cannot imagine what it must be like for a 5-year-old to go to school and learn that this language of family love, of mom, dad, grandma and grandpa, is bad. What must it feel like to be a small child and feel shame for your own mother's language? Five-year-olds read the world well and understand quickly that their family's language is bad. This is why they learn to say, "I don't speak Spanish." Shame does terrible things; anger follows shame. (This unlearning is not always comfortable.) I think when Tove raises this question with schools in the United States, she is moving us institutionally to problem posing. Traditionally, the dominant culture does not respond well to this type of probing, thoughtful activity.

Declaration: Kids Need to Learn.   Tove continues to campaign for the United Nations to adopt the Declaration of Children's Linguistic Human Rights. Before I share it, let me explain something about Tove to you. English is not her first, nor second, nor third language. Every time I ask her how many languages she speaks, reads, writes, and understands, we never get to the end of the answer. She always starts telling me stories about the languages along the way. I have noticed that she needs more than her own 10 fingers to do the counting. Even though English is not her first language, she is highly sensitive to gender-specific language that had, until recently, been so entrenched in the English language. In her writing, she has long used only the feminine pronoun as a little prod to help us move to a more equitable approach to gender-free language. I have some male friends who are very sensitive to this and really offended. Feels good to me.

Tove, like many of us, believes that kids need to learn. She noted early in her writing that we don't learn what we don't understand. Therefore, she is an international leader in persuading the United Nations to adopt the following declaration:

Declaration of Children's Linguistic Human Rights

1. Every child should have the right to identify with her original mother tongue and have her identification accepted and respected by others.
2. Every child should have the right to learn the mother tongue fully.
3. Every child should have the right to choose when she wants to use the mother tongue in all official situations.

One of the best experiences I ever had with this declaration happened with the departmental secretary/assistant. Sheri and I see and know in very different ways, but we laugh and have a great time learning together. Two years ago I remember when I first hung a laminated copy of this declaration on the wall above my desk. On more than one occasion, I was aware that Sheri was musing on it but not mentioning it. This week, as I was walking out the door, Sheri looked at it and quietly said, "Makes sense to me, Joan." I smiled and thought a lot about patience on my way home.

A Team and B Team.   Another idea of Tove's, which has affected critical pedagogy in North America, is her concept of the A Team and B Team. Tove speaks to the issues of power with this construct. The A Team, which controls the power and material resources, continually invalidates and marginalizes the voice of the B Team. This is the way the A Team socially constructs knowledge and maintains its own power.

Pada is a young Hmong-American woman. She has successfully finished her undergraduate studies, she has her teaching credentials, and she is now a graduate student. She told me a story about discovering the A and B teams when she arrived in the United States.

> *When I started high school in the United States, my achievement was high and my command of the English language fairly good. However, I was still terrified of all the tests the schools gave upon my entering. The first battery of tests was to determine which track was best for me: ESL track, B track, or A track. I was placed on the B track, which was designed to prepare students for a vocational career. I felt like the teachers thought I was incompetent. They gave us very little homework and hardly any real reading and real writing. I remember having to memorize lists of words and their definitions. I could see that the students in A track were always doing more interesting work; I could see that the A track was used to prepare people for college, which was my dream. Every time I tried to get into the A track, my counselor would remind me about my initial entry scores on the exams. I was achieving on B track, but that didn't seem to matter to anyone.*
>
> *During my second year of high school, my counselor finally allowed me to try A track. However, he continually discouraged me and made me bring letters of support from teachers in order to make the transfer. At that time in my life, I did not understand the meaning of words such as socialization practices, schooling, and teacher expectations, but I could understand that I was being programmed for less than my dream.*

Obviously, a society to which stratification into separate classes would be fatal must see to it that intellectual opportunities are accessible to all on equable and easy terms (Dewey, 1944, pp. 88-89). In spite of this early warning from Dewey, tracking continues (see Note 5). I wanted the students to read Dewey, to understand Dewey, to experience Dewey, so I decided to consciously create an A Team and a B Team on the first night of one of my classes. The experience was so powerful that it took us a few weeks to recover. The class of 38 arrived at 5 p.m. We were in a large room with all of the chairs screwed to the floor in straight rows that would surely horrify Dewey if he were alive today (see Note 6). The teachers/grad students drifted in and greeted each other. Those who knew me and had been in my classes before began by hugging friends, visiting, renewing friendships, and mostly moving towards the chairs in the front of the room. Before everyone was seated, I announced that those who had been in my classes before should sit in the front chairs, and those who had not should sit towards the back. Everyone immediately complied. The front of the room continued with happy noise; the back of the room became quieter. We started class, and I consciously directed my comments to those in the front of the room; those in the back received only token attention. For the next two hours, we continued like this: I would initiate an idea or a thought and ask the students to discuss it. After their discussion, I would ask for whole-group sharing, but I mostly called on only those in the front. I consciously tried to assign status, power, and prestige to those in the front. I behaved as if they *knew more* and as if their knowledge were *more valuable*. They thrived. The back of the room became quieter and quieter. Soon I was able to see angry, frustrated looks. During the small-group activities, I could tell they were sharing their anger with each other; I ignored it and walked among the students in the front of the room, who couldn't understand why I was making the new students feel so bad.

After the two hours, I couldn't take it any longer. The front of the room was confused; the back of the room angry. I asked how many of them were teachers; there were 38 teachers in the room. I asked them how many of them were involved with tracking in their class; 38 were involved with tracking. I asked why. The front and back explained to me that they had to do it because some students were *ahead of* and *knew more* than other students. They still did not see the connection to our class. I asked the names of the various tracks: yellow, red, green, blue. They all knew which students went in which track. I asked them if their assumptions about students made a difference in their students' achievement. The front and the back agreed: Our tracks reflect what the students knew.

Although I could tell by looking at their faces, I asked the back of the room how they were feeling: furious, angry, worthless, and finally, ready to drop the class. The front of the room still could not understand why I was making the new students feel so bad. Finally, I just told them that I had created an A Team and a B Team so they could experience it. *Experiencing* is different from *knowing about*. The students in this class are all teachers who *know about* tracking, but when they *experienced* it, they did not like it.

Tracking is so institutionalized in the geographical area where I live that the very thought of challenging it is almost considered heresy. Even the B Team in class that night wanted to legitimize it and rationalize it. Hegemony rears its ugly head again. It took three more classes of dialogue and reading and writing before I felt that the class had come together as a whole and could see that I had manipulated them and the context into the haves and the have-nots. I had consciously reproduced a reflection of their world and their individual classrooms. I had socially sorted on purpose to make a point that A Teams and B Teams always work to the advantage of the A Team. Five-year-olds know the difference between the buzzards and the blessed. It doesn't matter what color you label the track.

Lucille, an African American grad student, always knew her elementary teachers thought she was on the B Team, but when she was in junior college, she was amused to find she had been placed on yet another B Team. Only this time, it had a new name: the Lazy Tongues. She was placed in an ESL phonics class with Spanish, Chinese, and Japanese speakers. The professor referred to them as LEPs; Lucille and the other African Americans were the Lazy Tongues. Lucille now believes that this is the way her institution reproduced the existing superstructure, or the A Team and the B team.

What in the world does reproduction of the existing superstructure have to do with classroom teachers? Critical pedagogues often speak and write about schools maintaining and recreating social status and power. For example, if one group of students is labeled *gifted* and another group *limited*, which group benefits? I know a school that divides the *limiteds* into *low limiteds* and *high limiteds*. Apparently, the *high limiteds* would be the A Team of the B Team.

I think that we teachers often don't realize the role we play in this. We have a tendency to think that others do it, but not us. However, if we are creating (consciously or unconsciously) A Teams and B Teams in our classes, we are also a part of reproducing the existing social, cultural, and political power bases. How does this history of critical pedagogy relate to the everyday life of a classroom teacher? Look around your own school and ask yourself these questions:

1. Who is on the A Team and who is on the B Team? What part might I be playing in the reproduction and maintenance of the two teams?
2. Which students are meaningfully and purposefully interacting to generate more knowledge?
3. Who is doing fill-in-the-blank dittos? Why?
4. Am I unconsciously taking part in the selection and maintenance of the A Team at my school because of my silence?
5. Do we track? Why? Which track is best? Why?

Critical pedagogy relates fundamentally to every teacher and to every student every day. These are basic questions and issues that we live every day. However, many times we have been so schooled, so institutionalized to believe that we are helpless to make a difference in our own environment. If not us, who? Schools R Us? Critical pedagogy enables us to stop the *"yeah-buts"* and to begin to recognize our own power as professionals. Critical pedagogy gives us the power to understand that we must do the very best where we are today. We cannot fix every educational problem in the world, but we can live our own beliefs in our own communities. Critical pedagogy is the power that leads us from silence to voice.

I will conclude my introduction to Tove Skutnabb-Kangas with one last story. She and I keep a running list of who can find the most damaging, dreadful, despicable label. I have a new one that she has not seen but will when she reads this. I recently read a document that left our university and went to a state agency. In the document I found a new label under the category of diversity: It was *differing gender*. I guess that would be Tove and me, and it would place us on the B Team. Top that one, Tove!

I have a suspicion that the A Team/B Team is one of those metaphors that forces us to confront our own assumptions, our own experiences. We can agree on this: None of us supports the idea of the A Team and the B Team. However, I choose to acknowledge that it exists in multiple ways, and I will not deny that it has a long and painful history for some people. Critical pedagogy calls on us to name, to throw it on the table, and then provide a safe place where ALL can reflect on it, talk about it, and begin to deconstruct it. Only after this can we take action and build a more just society for all. Let the dialogue begin.

As I write this, I am reminded of the famous quotation by Frederick Douglass: Power concedes nothing without demand. It never did, and it never will (See Note 7).

VYGOTSKY

Who is this Russian psychologist who keeps reemerging in my life and tugging me to my next developmental level? Each time I remeet him, I relearn one of his most fundamental lessons: that which I can do with someone else today, I can do alone tomorrow. A small technicality before we continue: most of Russia is not in Europe, but for my purposes here, a close neighbor is good enough. Earlier I demonstrated how I had to use his legacy of thought and language before I was able to begin to internalize the language and thoughts of critical pedagogy. Figure 3.2 visualizes this process. Now I would like to tell you more about his ideas.

Why Vygotsky?

Vygotsky is just the person to tug us beyond tradition. He is just the person to lead us back to the future. The past is not bad; much can be learned from it (as in this particular case), but the past is just that—past—and as teachers, we have to teach tomorrow, not yesterday. Just as he did with his contemporaries, he can help us rethink our past practices, our present, and our future to ensure that our practices reflect today and tomorrow.

The broader the perspective we bring to ideas, the better the idea. Ideas are improved when people of highly diverse groups gather together and share their perspectives. The broader the representation, the better the democracy. We are called by the legacy of Vygotsky to surround and improve our ideas with a broad spectrum of critical thought (see Note 8).

As we experience global demographic shifts, a new social context compels us to regenerate theory and practice, thus creating our own personal praxis that informs and empowers teaching and learning in a diverse society. This search for philosophy and practice, which draws on the strengths of many cultures in society while promoting cognitive development from a critical perspective, leads to Lev Vygotsky (see Note 9).

Who Is This Educator from the Past Who Tugs Us into Our Future?

Vygotsky's legacy for critical education of today and tomorrow includes three main concepts:

> Sociocultural learning, or the context matters.
>
> The zone of proximal development, or our interaction with friends, in this context matters.
>
> The relationship between thought and language, or words and ideas used, in this context matters.

Sociocultural Learning

In a conversation about real estate, you may have heard about the importance of location, location, location. In teaching and learning, it is context, context, context. The next time you muse on the importance of context in your own teaching and learning, you can thank Vygotsky. For example, how does critical pedagogy play out in Hollywood, Hackensack, or Howes? Depends on context. Those who live within a community, those who have experienced a unique (social, historical, cultural, political) context, have understandings that others do not have. Students, teachers, and community members know their questions in distinctive ways; they generate their answers based on their own context. Their questions and answers can be informed from voices in other (social, cultural, historical, political) places, but ultimately context sways conclusions. Anyone who has ever raised

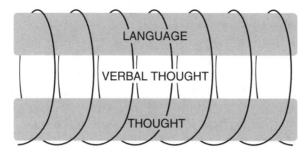

FIGURE 3.2 Visualization of the relationship between language and thought, based on Vygotsky

teenagers understands the major role that the environment plays in determining one's path.

We hear a lot about sociocultural learning lately, and it tends to have different names that all mean about the same thing: socially grounded learning, social learning, sociocultural-political-historical learning, etc. The basic point is that we generate knowledge in a social context. Learning is social and sometimes noisy. When we don't understand something, we visit with a friend and begin to understand better. What happens when you are sitting in a presentation, and you have been talked at, talked at, and talked at? You love it when the speaker finally finishes so you can visit with your friends about your ideas. I hope reading this book will make you want to talk about it in your own context. Learning is social.

The primacy of being human is how we use language in social contexts to make meaning. As we talk, we manipulate and mediate our language and our thoughts, which leads us to higher cognitive processes. As we talk, we get smarter, with a few notable exceptions that pop into my mind. All of the meaning that we generate and mediate is socially and culturally grounded. Teachers who understand this are guiding students, rather than transmitting knowledge. Students are actively generating knowledge rather than passively storing information for possible future use.

In the following picture of social learning, I will use the term *sociocultural learning* to portray the Vygotskian perspective. This picture of sociocultural learning will focus on Pablo, a sixth-grade migrant student from Mexico who is in school in the United States. The purpose of the following story is to view the classroom as an entity influenced by the larger world that surrounds each of our students.

Pablo.   In the back of the sixth-grade classroom, Pablo sat alone. His jacket covered his head to shut out the classroom and the world during the first 2 weeks of class. He did not speak to his new classmates, nor did they speak to

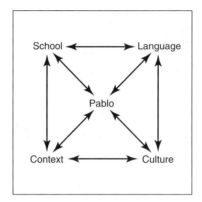

FIGURE 3.3   The world of Pablo

him. Any attempt by the teacher to draw him into interaction with others was met with resistance on his part, as well as on the part of the other students. The context of his life had influenced him, and likewise he influenced those around him. Much of the world had treated Pablo badly. Because he had been shifted from town to town, he did not want to make ties with anyone for fear that these ties would soon be broken by yet another move to a different school. Instead, he sat at his desk, using his jacket as a shield to isolate him from anyone who dared to get too close. Pablo is surrounded by many factors that touch his life (Figure 3.3). He is in the middle of a larger sociocultural context. The world has sent him many messages; he has read his world.

Some, in education, would blame Pablo for not doing his homework, for not sitting up straight, for not *caring* about learning. However, we cannot view Pablo in isolation; we have to look at all the influences that affect Pablo on a daily basis. This particular student cares a lot; it is just that no one in this school has learned it yet.

After many years of being moved from one teacher to another, in and out of resource and special education classes, Pablo found a home in a sixth-grade mainstream classroom. He was able to write only two- or three-word sentences when assisted by his teacher, Kathleen. In her classroom, students working collaboratively took on specific roles to complete the projects. These roles were frequently changed so that all students could realize equal status and the opportunity to lead their groups. High emphasis was placed on collaborating and valuing whatever abilities each student brought to the group, as well as arriving at consensus for group reports while maintaining individual accountability. Kathleen was aware that another student in the class, Angela, understood Pablo's language, his culture, and his world. Kathleen placed Pablo in a group of four students: Pablo, Angela, and two of the nicest English-dominant boys in her class. She believed that this combination of student resources would be the best possible social situation she could offer this troubled student.

At first, Pablo contributed very little, but taking the coat off his head and joining the group was a victory. Angela offered assistance to him during group activities, and she listened when he spoke.

The two other boys in the group were supportive and yet respectful of his space, and somehow understood that Pablo needed time. Soon, the four began to have fun in their group; they were creating their own group dynamic. After several weeks, Pablo started to take responsibility for himself and his group. Angela translated when necessary, but the group was more and more often focused on the problem-solving activities, and they made meaning in their own way.

Pablo finally removed his coat during class. He next volunteered to be the reporter so he could relate the group findings aloud in front of the class.

Initially, he reported with some prompting from Angela. Later, he was able to complete an individual report of their project alone, rather than having to ask for Angela's assistance. After his interactive work in the safe environment of his group, Pablo was able to construct his own paragraph of five sentences based on what he had learned during the activity. Group learning does not always work for all students, but sometimes it can be very helpful, as in this case.

Pablo eventually worked at levels others had not thought possible. The sociocultural context of the class had a powerful effect on Pablo and his learning. Not only did Pablo construct his knowledge in this classroom, but he was able to begin to reconstruct his world.

When I last saw Pablo, he had moved on to seventh grade at the junior high school. I was driving by his school in the afternoon while students were outside waiting for school buses to take them home. There stood Pablo, alone, in the blistering valley heat, with his coat tightly zipped up, as if to close off the world. Once again the sociocultural context of Pablo had placed in him a vulnerable position. He tightly pulled his coat around his shoulders to protect himself from influences of his new educational world. Sadly, I watched Pablo and was reminded that if we are to reach our potential as a society, each Pablo must have an opportunity to realize maximum potential. Teachers often ask, "What can I do?" Pablo and Vygotsky provide part of the answer. The interrelationship of all students and all languages in a safe and secure environment is fundamentally important for literacy and cognitive development. It is also important for our future. (Wink, Putney, & Bravo-Lawrence, January/February, 1995).

Zone of Proximal Development

What in the world is the zone of proximal development (ZPD)? Once again, we can turn to Vygotsky and Pablo to discover the answer:

> The ZPD is the distance between the actual developmental level as determined by independent problem solving and the level of potential development as determined through problem solving under adult guidance or in collaboration with more capable peers.
> (Vygotsky, 1978, p. 86)

Pablo's Story: the ZPD in Action

> First, no one thought he could learn.
> Second, he learned with his group.
> Third, he was able to learn alone.

Vygotsky viewed experience as a key factor affecting the relationship between thought and speech. Students use language to communicate thoughts, and through the social act of verbalizing those thoughts (talking to each other) combine their experiences with those of others. These zones we create in our classes, in our departments, in our communities, and in our homes make a difference in individual lives and in society. They have the potential to lead to self and social transformation.

Thought and Language

The third legacy of Vygotsky relates to the powerful interrelationship between thought and language. The eighth graders in the following example demonstrate the ways in which students use their language to generate thoughts and how the thoughts affect their language. Words and ideas: it's a two-way street.

Richard: An Example from Secondary. Richard's social studies class was studying the Preamble to the Constitution. In this classroom of 28 students, 15 are English-dominant, 6 are Spanish-dominant, 4 are Cambodian-dominant, and 3 are Lao-dominant. The text and the language of the class-room are English. Richard and his students have just orally read the Preamble in English. After heterogeneously grouping the students, Richard, the teacher, explained the assignment:

> *"Rewrite the Preamble using your own language. Look at the Preamble, pick it apart, and put the thoughts back together with any language that you want to use. Words like everyday talk at home or outside of school, Spanish, English, Cambodian, Lao. Use street language if you want. Use any language, but just demonstrate the thoughts of the Preamble. Afterwards, in your groups, redo it in English so that I can understand."*
>
> *"Our language? Any language? Just write the ideas?" the students asked.*
>
> *They buzzed with each other about the prospect of writing their thoughts in their languages and then translating them to English.*
>
> *Richard answered, "Write it, agree on it as a group, read it, and explain it. Brainstorm. Put your homo sapiens' cabezas together. How would you put this in everyday language so you can go to the local market and talk about the Constitution?" After a pause he prompted, "We the people, me and my friends."*
>
> *"Me and my posse?" asked one.*
>
> *"Yes!"*
>
> *"Yo y mis amigos?"*
>
> *"Si."*
>
> *"My buds and I?"*
>
> *"Sure."*

(Putney, L. 1993, pp. 48–49)

The purpose of this lesson is for the students to relate the language of the Preamble with the embedded thoughts. Marginalized students are often denied the opportunity of full participation in discussing abstract concepts in content areas. In the previous example, Richard organized his classroom and implemented his own pedagogy so all students internalized the abstract concepts of this social studies class. Richard was building on the resources that each student brings to the classroom.

As the students write and talk in their own language they internalize the democratic ideas of the Constitution. This process is multidimensional, boundless, dynamic, and noisy. Language informs thought, and thoughts come to life in language.

In a pluralistic society, the issue of language acquisition is fundamental for all teachers. If students don't get to read and talk in a language they know, they don't get to learn. Using our own language makes us smarter, which is why everyone in the world loves her own language. And, when we are smarter, we learn other languages faster. Language develops cognition; words turn into thoughts, and thoughts turn into more words. All students need to talk and listen to each other in social, academic, and problem-solving contexts. Vygotsky's concept of the relationship between thought and language is how I developed my own cognition about critical pedagogy.

Vygotsky's Legacy to Critical Pedagogy

Meaningful dialogue matters.
Our lived experiences make a difference.
Our business is to keep tugging students
to their next cognitive level.
The combination of words and ideas generates
more.

What does a Vygotskian Class Look Like? An Example from Postsecondary.   It has been my experience that sometimes teachers might teach about Vygotsky but not adapt their own personal pedagogy to create a context whereby students experience a Vygotskian classroom. Following is a description of a postsecondary classroom that had the experience but did not see it, nor recognize it, until they articulated it (LeAnn Putney, personal communication, December 15, 1998):

> *"What does a Vygotskian class look like?" the graduate student asked after they had studied Vygotsky.*
> *"Well, what have we been doing since day one of class in this course?" the professor replied.*
> *"We keep an issues log each night as we read our assignments," the first student replied.*
> *"Then, when we get to class, we sit in small groups and discuss the issues each of us has highlighted," replied the second student.*
> *"Next, our whole class discussion is determined by the our logs, not from the text and not from your log," the third graduate student said to the professor.*
> *"How did we create the midterm project?" the professor asked the class.*

"Oh, yeah," the first student replied, "I remember that we created six different possibilities for a midterm, and each student could choose one. Some of us renegotiated our choices a couple of times."

"How did we decide to grade the various projects?" the faculty member queried.

"We created a rubric together one night in class," a student answered.

"I remember that some of us read the same difficult journal article, then got together and talked about it, and then presented it for our colleagues in class," another student shared.

"I knew when I assigned those readings that on an individual basis they might be a bit beyond you because you would be grappling with new academic thought and language. But I remember that each group had a dynamite demonstration of the materials so that your colleagues could do their own sense-making of those same articles. Together, it seems that you have extracted meaning from some very heavy readings that you all complained about from the first day," the professor said, and the students smiled knowingly.

"And look at how much we learned," the professor concluded. "Now my question of you is: What will you do with the new knowledge you have generated?"

THE NORTH AMERICAN VOICE

When the Latin and European critical perspective arrived in the United States, it was nourished by two schools of thought that had a long history in North American educational theory: reconstructionism and progressivism. A critical educational approach had a waiting audience of those who believed that the purpose of education was to continually reconstruct society. Critical theory and Freirian thought joined with democratic ideals, which were central to progressivism. Social reform was inherent in the improvement of schools. The Latino and European critical perspective shared with the progressivists a belief that all of education is value-laden and morally-grounded. Dewey's progressive ideas were fertile ground for the seed of critical theory from Europe and Latin America (see Note 10). Not only did Dewey's idea connect tightly with critical theory, but also with democracy (see Note 11). Dewey saw the connections between democracy and pedagogy. Democracy was not a subject to be studied, but rather a value to be lived. Dewey believed that the theory and practice of democracy should be nourished by the power of pedagogy. Books are filled with personal stories of Dewey (see

Note 12) that bring him to life and show how he turned his beliefs into behaviors everyday. In what follows my goal is to bring to life the legacy of Dewey as it might actually be experienced in schools today.

Dewey

Dewey said it best: "Accept the child where the child is." Critical pedagogy of today in North America is grounded in this legacy from Dewey. If we could all remember this simple educational principle, how much better our system would be. But sometimes we forget. The following is a description of a family night at the beginning of the school year for the first graders. During the evening, one of the parents asked the teacher

> PARENT: Where do you begin? Do you begin with what the students know?
>
> TEACHER: Oh no, we start on chapter 4; the first three chapters are just review, and I don't want to waste my time with that. If the students aren't there yet, they don't belong in my class.

Run, families, run! I know that this teacher studied Dewey in her credential program. She forgot. We continue to forget another lesson from Dewey: "Accept the child as the child is."

> K TEACHER: I just don't know what else to do. Esmeralda just sits there. She never says anything. She never takes part in any "regular" activities. She would rather sit alone in her seat all day, I guess.
>
> TEACHER #2: Well, she would do better if she could speak English.
>
> K TEACHER: All the students would do better if they came to school speaking English. In any case, our jobs would be easier.
>
> TEACHER #2: Still, you would think that Esmeralda's parents would teach her English. But, I guess that's supposed to be our problem, too.

Accepting who the students are is sometimes very difficult for teachers. Sometimes teachers don't want the students of today; they want the students of yesterday. It's not going to happen. I think that Dewey meant for us to accept the whole child whatever race, class, gender, language, culture. When teachers can't accept who the child is, they sometimes want to blame it on others, such as the child or parents. I think this tells us more about the teacher than the child and the parents.

Every educator has studied the effects of progressivism and reproduction on the educational system. These are not abstract, historical ideas that can be relegated to a history book, placed on a shelf, and forgotten. These ideas are alive and well today in a new form with a broader historical, cultural, and political base.

Oftentimes, simultaneous and conflicting ideologies move through history together, yet another contradiction as we experience change. Today, we would call this polarization; however, it is not a new phenomenon. During the days of progressivism and reconstructionism, very divergent ideas existed at the same time. Critical pedagogy often refers to oppositional views as the "other," which is reflected in the way that schools were historically used to control and to maintain the existing power structure. This is not a new concept on the North American continent. As early as the 1850s, schools were considered to be the most effective method of Americanizing the many immigrants who were coming to the New World for freedom and democracy. Many believed it was the responsibility of the schools, with their European American philosophies, to test the loyalty of "new immigrants," who were the groups who tended to come from southern and eastern Europe and Asia. I immediately can think of several new immigrants I know whose loyalty is being tested today. Can you? Cubberley of Stanford was an eloquent leader of this movement. He felt that to Americanize was to Anglicize. It was the duty of the schools to assimilate the new immigrants as part of the American race (Cremin, 1964). American race? What in the world is that? "Americanism is not, and never was, a matter of race or ancestry" (Roosevelt, as cited in Carnes, 1995) (see Note 13).

The social relations of power that take place in schools every day mirror the power relationships of society. It seems we, in schools, are trying to do the same thing. Bowles and Gintis (1976) wrote that there is a simple correspondence between schooling, class, family, and social inequities. Schools are mirrors of society.

The idea of schools reproducing inequalities of society is a part of the critical theory legacy to the North American school of today. It is not always an easy, nor welcome, topic for discussion; sometimes it causes great resistance. However, I would ask only that we follow the advice of Goodlad (in Goldberg, 1995), who was reflecting on the words of John Dewey, who said: "What the researcher in education must do is to get immersed in the complex phenomena, then withdraw and think about the issues" (p. 85).

Ada

Alma Flor Ada has influenced multiple classrooms and families with her critical approach to teaching and learning. Her influences are particularly felt on the West coast.

I know we aren't supposed to say this, but Alma Flor Ada empowers me. After I am with her, I am braver, smarter, and nicer. She lives her beliefs daily and somehow makes it okay to be whoever you happen to be. In addition, I never go in front of a group to teach unless I have her methodology (Ada, 1988a, 1988b) safely tucked away in the corner of my brain. She calls it the Creative Reading Method, which is far too narrow a description for me. I have found it to be effective in any teaching/learning context.

Instead of the five-step lesson plan, try her approach:

- Descriptive Phase: information is shared by teacher, text, media, etc.
- Personal Interpretation Phase: students grapple with new information based on their lived experiences.
- Critical Phase: invites reflection and critical analysis.
- Creative Phase: theory to practice connects learning from class to the real world of the student.

I find that these four phases are effective whether I am with 5-year-olds, 15-year-olds, or 55-year-olds. Of course, it need not be a lock-step, linear approach. Rather, it ebbs and flows as students acquire and inquire into new knowledge while they (and we) continually move through learning-relearning-unlearning. This pedagogical process ends with creation/action and then begins again. The students find ways to live the ideas, to create more ideas, or take the ideas to their own real world. It is an approach that any teacher can begin tomorrow. If you are accustomed to lecturing or only following a perspective lessons design, this teaching/learning experience requires only two things: courage and patience. As we enter into transformative pedagogy, it is often difficult to know exactly where to start. Alma Flor's process of the descriptive, personal interpretive, critical, and creative phases provides classroom teachers with a framework in which to discover their own praxis. Try it. However, when you are teaching and learning with this approach, remember what Alma Flor answered (March 20, 1998) when asked how-to-do critical pedagogy: "I am going to quote my daughter who says that the only way to do it is to deeply, deeply believe in the learner (see Note 14).

McCaleb

How many times have we heard educators say, *"I schedule parent conferences, but the parents won't come. How do we 'do' parental involvement?"* Sudia Paloma McCaleb (1994) is helping educators build community and build books. She asks educators to look within and examine their own assumptions about families and literacies. Recently, a secondary teacher read this book and said to me:

> *I used to think that "these" families were illiterate and didn't care. Now I know that my assumptions contributed to keeping the families from coming to visit with me.*

For McCaleb, transformative educators are those who view the role of a teacher not as the all-knowing instructor, but rather as a coparticipant in the learning process with students. A Spanish-English bilingual secondary teacher told me:

> *I held parent conferences last year, and not a single parent came. I thought I had been accessible to parents. However, McCaleb made me realize that the families were actually isolated by the appointment system, yet another hidden gatekeeping process. There I sat in my room alone, while Spanish-speaking families were to make appointments in the front office with a secretary who spoke only English.*
>
> *This year I contacted all the parents and invited them to our first family night. I promised them I would get all notices to them in Spanish, and I gave them the name and phone number of a Spanish-speaking secretary. During the next conference schedule, more than 50 percent of the families came to visit during class, and three parents called later. My goal is get all the parents to come.*

Giroux

I have written of the importance of courage and patience in our study of critical pedagogy. You will need both when you begin to read Peter McLaren and Henry Giroux. I was reminded of a raging river on a stormy day when I first read these two critical theorists. Behind those big words you will indeed find big ideas.

The first time I ever read the words of Henry Giroux, I actually thought the book was vibrating. I had never read that type of language, but I must have been ready for those powerful ideas. I could not put the book down. Even as I remember it today, it is like an almost physical and metaphysical experience. I finally got it! We, as teachers, are not to be passive, robotic technocrats who can't do anything because of the administration, or the texts, or the parents, or the students, or the tests. We are to be intellectuals and professionals who take control of our own teaching and learning. Perhaps we can't control society's perception of teachers as *less*, but we can control how we perceive ourselves. My suspicion is that as we begin to come to know ourselves as intellectuals and professionals and turn those beliefs into behaviors, society will begin to change its perception of us.

Giroux's idea of correspondence, which states that schooling functions to reproduce the class structure of the workplace, reaches back to the thinking of the Frankfurt School's theory of reproduction and to the economic production ideas of Marx. Giroux suggests that even though our roots are in the theory of reproduction and resistance, it is time to move to the *possible* that lies within each of us. He focuses his critical lens on curriculum, which is generated by the students and teachers and reflects their real world. Building from the Freirian concept, Giroux (1988) states that curriculum is never just a neutral body, a warehouse of knowledge. Rather, curriculum is a way of organizing knowledge, values, relationships of social power. Every time I hear a teacher say, "Yeahbut, the curriculum we have to use is so bad," I hear the words of Giroux in my head. He challenges us to challenge ourselves. We are not passive technocrats devoid of power over curriculum. If the curriculum needs to be challenged, challenge it. If not us, who?

McLaren

Peter McLaren challenges teachers to be courageous moral leaders who understand how knowledge, language, experience, and power are central to society and our classrooms. He asks us to look again with new eyes and see how literacies are used to support the A Team. His theory crystallizes the concept that what we do as teachers is morally and ethically grounded. Students' lives are at stake daily in our practice. It matters what we do, and we can do a lot. McLaren's words are an echo of Dewey, who stressed the acceptance of the children on their own terms. Many have written of the teachable moment, but only Peter has described the teachable heart.

In the works of McLaren and Giroux, we continually find an underlying current of the potential in each of us. If you are courageous and patient enough in your reading of their ideas, you will find the hidden "yes-we-can" message they are sending us. It is this idea that transforms teachers to take action and causes the shift to social and self-transformation. They open the door to Freire's conscientization. How ironic that Giroux and McLaren, who are often viewed as theorists, can be the trigger to help us turn our own theory into action.

A Teachable Heart.   When I first heard McLaren (1994) mention this idea, I thought, "Yes, that is the by-product of good teaching and learning." I would like to say that he taught this to me, but really what he did is just affirm what I had previously learned from José of the Tucson phone book fame.

You will remember that José was one of that group of students who taught and learned with me for 6 consecutive years in Benson. The first year I met José he was in 7th grade and didn't say a word all year; José was very much like an ethnographer in that he participated in and observed everything. José was, and is, a quiet, private, and reserved person. In the 8th grade, José started to talk. In the 9th grade, he spoke, and students in the class began to listen. In 10th grade, students in other parts of the high school started to listen. In 11th grade, the students in student government started to listen. In 12th grade, the entire community started to listen when he graduated with honors in two languages.

In the spring of his senior year, the students chose to take a standardized national honors test in Spanish and in English so those with high achievement could be given college credit for their knowledge.

One of our most memorable teaching/learning experiences had taken place when he was a freshman in high school. One of his classmates had innocently asked how to say "I love you" in Spanish. In French? In German? In Swahili? The list went on and on. This was a turning point for all of us because we stopped whatever we were covering and began to research answers for the questions. For the next several weeks, the students went to libraries, interviewed travelers, and visited with families who had come from other countries. The students could not collect enough information to satisfy them; I was almost running to catch up as I tried to understand what was happening. Of course, we learned more about languages, and cultures, and geography than anything else could have taught us. The students also established a list of 25 different ways to say "I love you." They relished practicing in and out of class. Since that time, I have never been afraid to follow the natural curiosity of students.

Although this activity had not been mentioned in class since their freshman year, when José and his classmates sat down to take the national test, I wanted to include some part of it as a reminder of our very special time together. On the final page of the very long test, I had written in bold letters down the middle of the page:

Translate into as many languages as you can:

I love you. _____

I love you. _____

I love you. _____

I love you. _____

I love you. _____

I love you. _____

I love you. _____

I love you. _____

I love you. _____

I love you. _____

I love you. _____

I love you. _____

I love you. _____

As the students came to the end of the test, I could tell by the look on their faces that I had found the perfect parting memory for us. José was sitting in the middle row, the middle seat, as I quietly walked the rows during the test. When I came up behind him, I looked down at his paper and saw that he had written:

Yo sé.
Yo sé.
Yo sé.
Yo sé.
Yo sé.
Yo sé.
Yo sé.
Yo sé.
Yo sé.
Yo sé.
Yo sé.
Yo sé.
Yo sé.

Yo sé in English means I know.

From that moment on I have understood the importance of the teachable heart. José had one; he learned not only what was taught, but much more. And along the way he taught us all.

Cummins

Jim Cummins's concept of empowerment (1989), which has been used and abused by many, still focuses us on the primacy of power in educational and societal issues. Cummins has taught us that unless we ourselves are empowered, we cannot be involved with any other processes of empowerment. To be voiceless is to be powerless. If we view ourselves as helpless, we are. We cannot control how others have traditionally perceived us, but we can control how we perceive ourselves. Critical pedagogy empowers our theory and action into a personal praxis that challenges the exclusive membership of the A Team.

Empowerment Framework.   Schools often ask, What can we do? I feel Cummins's framework is vastly underrated and underused. Everyone talks about it as a marvelous theoretical construct, but very few do it. I suggest that it is highly doable—tomorrow! It doesn't cost anything; you won't need a mandate; you won't need a committee, or another spiral notebook for your shelf. Just do it.

The beauty of this model is that it is highly adaptable in any context. As seen in Figure 3.4, Cummins provides guidelines along a powerful path of intervention. It is not a prescribed recipe. Teachers and learners need to bring their knowledge and experience to the model and adapt it to fit their own particular context. Schools and communities can begin the dialogue by examining their own perspectives on Cummins's framework. The following questions, which are all based on Cummins's four areas of the empowerment model, can be used for teachers, students, administrators, and/or community members. All you need to do is bring the community together and let the dialogue begin.

1. *Cultural and linguistic incorporation:* Is our theory and practice additive or subtractive? Why? What does that mean? How can we learn? Are all students encouraged to keep their family's culture and to learn more about other cultures too? What does multicultural mean? What does it mean to me? In what ways do we show respect for all cultures and languages? Do kids come into our schools speaking more than one language and leave 12 years later speaking only one? Why? Does our practice reflect our theory?

FIGURE 3.4   Framework for intervention

Source: From Empowering Minority Students, by J. Cummins, 1989, Sacramento: California Association for Bilingual Education. Copyright 1989 by the California Association for Bilingual Education. Reprinted by permission.

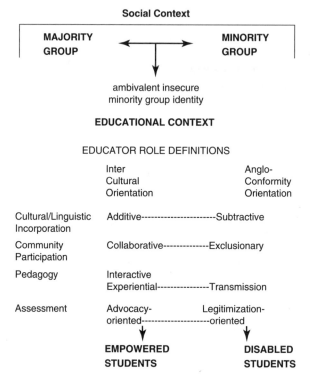

2. *Community participation:* Do all families feel included in the school processes? Who does? Who doesn't? How can we learn what families really feel about their inclusion or exclusion? What specific collaborative processes do we have? Who comes? Who doesn't come? Why?
3. *Pedagogy:* What does pedagogy mean? How can we learn? What type of learning do we believe in? Why? Are those beliefs turned into behaviors in our classrooms? How? Do the students really get to interact and experience their own generation of knowledge, or are they just memorizing facts that may soon be dated? What can we do?
4. *Assessment of programs:* When we talk about the programs in our schools, do we find ourselves legitimizing or advocating? What is the difference? How can we learn? What specific programs make me feel like advocating? Why? We always assess our students, but do we ever assess our own role in our local education? Should we? How? Why?

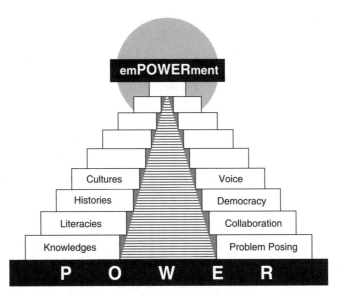

FIGURE 3.5   Putting the power back in emPOWERment

This process of reflection and action leads to empowerment. My only cautionary note for those who plan to examine critically Cummins' empowerment framework is this: Allow plenty of time and be supportive of each other and the process. This is not a 3-hour inservice program. Allow at least a year for the reflective phase and another year for the action. Things will change.

I suspect there are two reasons people don't actually *do* the empowerment framework. First, it seems too simple. How could that possibly work? Don't be fooled. The empowerment framework is not simple, nor is it simplistic. Its merit lies in the fact that it is grounded in highly complex theory and, at the same time, provides a clear picture of action. The four components force us all to confront ourselves as educators and to take the responsibility for our own educational actions. The second reason I think people tend to overlook this framework is because of the connotations of elite jargon that have developed around the "E" word. Okay, I'll say it: "Empowerment. Empowerment. Empowerment." Power is not something to be trivialized. I suggest that we put the power back in empowerment, as demonstrated in Figure 3.5. Jim has joined with Tove to say clearly, "Power is, after all, what it is all about" (Skutnabb-Kangas & Cummins, 1988, p. 390).

The meaning of empowerment is not fixed; it is constantly emerging and redefining itself; its definition is daily informed by teachers and students as they explore its boundaries. However, the primacy of empowerment is power.

In the same way that Peter McLaren has consistently warned us of the insidious danger of critical pedagogy being reduced to nothing more than banal liberal education, Jim Cummins has warned us of the abuse of multicultural education as it becomes nothing more than celebrations of festivals and foods. I far prefer the directness of Cummins's *antiracist, antisexist, anticlassist* education, which forces all educators to confront the real issues of our own involvement in the hidden (and not so hidden) processes of institutionalized racism.

Cummins's concept of empowerment (1989) expanded (1996) to include the concept of negotiating identities, which is exactly what we *do* when we *do* critical pedagogy. Cummins has backed away from the term, *empowerment,* because of its patronizing use in some circles. Empower is not a transitive verb; it does not take a direct object. Think about it: If you say that you empower someone else, who controls the power?

Here is the point of negotiating identities: ". . . human relationships are at the heart of schooling (Cummins, 1996, p. 1). What we do matters. The connections we create in classrooms are central to students' growth as they negotiate their own identities—and we, while learning with them, continually negotiate our own identities. These interactions trigger a process whereby students create their own sense of self. Furthermore, these human relationships can have a negative or positive effect. The implications throughout Cummins (1996) are clear: Students may be failing, not because of *who they are,* but rather because of *what is being* communicated to them by their teachers. These human interactions are the ways we negotiate identities in our classrooms. These relationships are evident when students transform their own self-image and discover who they are and can be and thus create the future for all of us.

None of this takes place in a vacuum. These new and emerging identities are surrounded by the powerful relationships between teachers and students. In your classroom. In my classroom. We are a part of our own personal pedagogy. It's true: We are in the classroom, too. It is not about them; it is about us. The vision of critical pedagogy makes clear our own human potential and that of every student in our classroom. Just as in 1989 we all tried to understand and explain empowerment, so once again we will all now be called upon to clarify negotiating identities. Cummins says that human relationships are the ways we negotiate identities in our classrooms. These relationships are evident when students transform their own self-image, discover who they are, and redefine themselves, and thus creating the future.

Collaborative and Coercive Relations of Power.   Cummins has continued to expand his ideas of power and empowerment with his concepts of coercive relations of power and collaborative relations of power (Cummins, 1994). We all have experienced coercive relations of power in which it is assumed there is a limited amount of power; power is fixed and subtractive. If one person gets more, the fear is that someone else must get less. These assumptions are nonsense. Power and problems have something in common: There is enough for us all. I have noticed that every time I mention this to a group of educators, there is always a knowing smile of understanding upon hearing that specific language. Well, let me be precise: most smile, a few squirm. What does that tell me? Who smiles? And who squirms? I think you know the answers to these questions.

When you have worked in a coercive environment, how did you feel? Were you effective? Productive? Not me. When I am in coercive environments, I do less, and I do it with anger. Collaborative relations of power assume that power is infinite; it grows and generates during collaborative interactions. When I have been in an environment of collaborative relations of power, I do more, better. The trick for teachers is to have the courage to negotiate their own power even when they are within the context of coercive relations of power.

Krashen

> *"Joan, why are you here for a reading conference?" he asked when he saw me at a large international airport.*
> *"Yes, we thought you were working in bilingual education. Have you changed?" his friend added.*

The airport was packed with teachers and principals all rushing to catch their flights after a large and very successful conference on literacy. It seemed that everyone in the airport was carrying the same colorful conference book bag filled with the books and memories of a truly stellar conference. As I was running to catch my plane, I happened to meet two former colleagues who knew me in another time and place. They seemed happy to see me, but were mystified: Why in the world would I be at a literacy conference?

Literacy is what it is all about. For all of us. If you are in education—any phase of education—you are involved with literacy, even we who have a history in bilingual and multilingual education.

Steve Krashen has done more to bring us all together around books than anyone else I can name. Books are about literacy. If critical pedagogy is about self and social transformation, he is a critical pedagogue. His gentle, humorous, and persistent voice continues to link all educators: those from the mainstream, with those from bilingual, with those from immersion, with those from ESL, with those from special education, with those from gifted programs. Pre-K; primary; elementary; middle school; high school; postsecondary; grad school: It doesn't matter. We are all involved with literacy development, which is the road to knowledge, new knowledge, and the unknown future. Of course, I am involved with literacy. So are you.

A national debate is taking place about literacy: How do kids learn to read? Is it better to focus on parts (for example, sounds)—or should we focus on the whole (for example, a story)? Which way is best? Well, it turns out that there is no one-size-fits-all; Jonathan taught me that. There is no one perfect way; my own kids taught me that. Just because I learned to read through phonics does not mean that it worked for them. In fact, it didn't. They learned in the exact opposite way: they read books, borrowed books, and slept with books. They loved books, something that eluded me and my sound-centric approach until I started reading to them when they were babies. However, access to books is the bottom line. Kids who have books have a far greater chance of learning to read and loving to read and continuing to read (See Note 15).

In spite of this, some states and districts are now mandating a one-way-only-approach to reading. Some teachers are now mandated to give so many teeny, tiny parts that there is no whole, thus creating a hole in literacy development. It is possible now to walk into schools and hear kids in multiple classrooms making the same sounds, from the same page, at the exact same time of day. If I hadn't actually experienced this, I doubt anyone could convince me of this reality.

> *"I can't believe I just told that student to stop reading and start doing the sounds with us," the teacher said to me. "She was sitting over in a chair completely enthralled in her book, and I stopped her from reading to do isolated sounds with us."*
>
> *"Why?" I asked.*
>
> *"Because if anyone walks by and sees one student not doing sounds in isolation with us, it will be written negatively on my evaluation," she sadly told me.*

And I will tell you, dear readers, that this is not an isolated example. I can cite many, many more from my own personal experience within the last academic year. If anyone had told me 2 years ago that it would come to this, I never would have believed it.

Yes, kids can learn to recite sounds, but can they read a good book? Do they *want* to read a good book? Do they have *access* to good books? Will they love to read? These are important questions. And even more important: Will they take a flashlight to bed with them? (See Note 16.)

The Benson Kids

Critical pedagogy always begins with questions. In the search for my own unique voice within the framework of critical pedagogy, I asked, "Where in the world does it come from?" These philosophical roots originated in many areas of the world and from multiple voices. These voices of culture, experience, language, knowledge, and power provide us with a foundation for further learning. I have painted a picture of the roots, which extend into the South and East. In addition, I have written of critical roots on the North American continent that have touched my life. This picture is not all-inclusive, but my wish is that it is enough to peak your curiosity and make you run, buy, or borrow another book.

However, if you really want to know where I learned about critical pedagogy, it was from those Benson kids. They were the ones who taught me all of this. The University of Arizona and Texas A&M think that they taught me this, but they only affirmed what students had taught me. I started out with the intention of teaching the Benson kids how to conjugate verbs; they taught me how to teach and learn. These students challenged all the philosophy and methodology that I had previously been taught. Now when I read roaring, raging books of theory, I see the faces of the students who taught me.

In the next chapter, I will ask the question, "Critical Pedagogy: How in the World Do You Do It?" I suspect that the following chapter will require all of my courage and most of your patience.

LOOKING AHEAD FOR NEW LEADERS: YOU!

Our future together will need new leaders. What critical leadership qualities do you bring to the future?

NOTES

1. For a more thorough discussion of bilingual education from a critical perspective, read Moraes (1996). She also has a wonderful chapter that looks at a bilingual education and immersion. O'Cadiz, Lindquist Wong, & Torres (1998) extend this discussion to social movements and curriculum with an emphasis on the Freirian concept of interdisciplinary teaching and learning throughout curriculum and across teacher education.

2. Many of the references listed in these chapter notes and in the bibliography have more on labels and categories as we all grow and seek language that is meaningful but not limiting. Campbell (1996) has a short section on language and ethnicity that adds to this discussion.

3. You may have noticed that I enjoy knowing about people while I am learning about their ideas. In this little book, I cannot tell all the stories about the people I mention. However, if you want to know about the amazing life of Gramsci, please read Csikszentmihalyi (1997).

4. For more on Marx and the concept of economic and social reproduction, please see deMarrais & LeCompte (1999) and any of the three editions of McLaren's *Life in Schools: An Introduction to Critical Pedagogy in the Foundations of Education.*

5. Tracking. For further reading on this subject, read Jeannie Oakes (1985). Tracking is also a recurring theme with the marvelous Milwaukee group of teachers and their newsletters, *Rethinking Schools.* (Rethinking Schools, 1001 East Keefe Avenue, Milwaukee, Wisconsin 53212; tel.: 414-964-9646; fax: 414-964-7220.)

6. "Here Lies the Man Who Convinced Americans to Unbolt School Desks from the Floor" is an old joke about Dewey's headstone for his grave. For more on this, read Newman (1998).

7. I was reminded of this quotation in Campbell (1996; p. 303).

8. For a more thorough discussion of the relationship between Freire and Vygotsky, I encourage you to read Christian Faltis (1990). In this article, Faltis explains that Freire's emphasis on critical reflection and action encourages teachers and students to talk about things that really matter to them. Purposeful social interaction in a classroom will open the door to more language and learning. Vygotsky's legacy of a theoretical framework grounded in the social nature of learning involves the negotiation of meaning through dialogue. When these two perspectives come together, teachers have the opportunity of turning theory into practice on a daily basis with students who are involved with language and learning—thus, with all students!

9. The first time I read Vygotsky was more than 30 years ago. At that time, his message rang clear and true for me. Throughout my life, his writings

have continued to find me. Within the last 10 years, my understanding of Vygotsky has been enriched by my colleague and friend, LeAnn Putney of University of Las Vegas. Her understandings of Vygotsky have been informed by her colleagues and friends at the University of California, Santa Barbara. What began as a conversation over coffee with LeAnn a decade ago has grown into sociocultural network of learning, relearning, and unlearning. I am indebted to this ever-growing zone of proximal development. For more on what I am learning, read Putney, et al. (1999).

10. For more on the connections between Dewey and Freire, I refer you to Campbell (1996).

11. Remember it this way: Dewey and democracy. For more on this, I refer you to Dewey (1944).

12. Newman (1998) captures Dewey, the man and legacy, with his fresh look at memorable old stories that education students so often hear and tell.

13. Newman (1998) also re-examines Cubberley with a focus on relearning and unlearning some of our historical educational assumptions.

14. This quotation from Alma Flor's daughter is a direct reference to Freeman & Freeman (1998), (1994), and (1992). The idea that teachers need to have faith in the learners is fundamental in their work. Freeman & Freeman (1998) have devoted their entire Chapter 10 to how-to-do it and why it matters.

15. For the most comprehensive information on *real* stats on *real* reading, I refer you to the latest Krashen publications in the bibliography and also to Jeff McQuillan (1998b). If critical pedagogy is about exploding myths (Nieto, 1996), and that certainly has been my experience, these specific references may very well explode a few more.

16. Finding my own kids in bed with books and flashlights was one of my most reassuring parental experiences. I didn't know the research then, but I sensed that this was a "good" problem. Since that time, we have learned a lot about kids and flashlights and books. Krashen (1993) finds that the data reflect that free readers have a chance. You might also like to read Quindlen (1998) who tells the story of the practice, not the theory.

chapter 4

Critical Pedagogy
How in the World Do You Do It?

Always think about practice.
A fundamental Freirian principle as expressed by Gadotti

THINKING ABOUT PRACTICE

Here I sit thinking about practice. Thinking about what can't be written: How to *do* critical pedagogy. In the previous chapters, we have discussed the meaning and the history of critical pedagogy. In this chapter I will move to a harder question:

How in the world do you *do* critical pedagogy? Is there a blueprint? A prescription? A recipe? Of course not, which will make writing this chapter fairly problematic. This must be how Mem Fox (1993) felt when she wrote about trying to teach what can't be taught. I am writing about what can't be written. I doubt I can teach someone how to *do* critical pedagogy. We do not *do* critical pedagogy; we *live* it. Critical pedagogy is not a method; it is a way of life (Jasso & Jasso, 1995).

My view of *living* critical pedagogy, however, is balanced by the persistent voice of Dawn Wink, who keeps rolling her eyes and saying:

"Yeahbut how, Mom?"

If you are one of the practitioners who constantly asks *how,* you will be glad to know that I have suffered a lot in the preparation of this chapter. Whenever I try to explain to someone that you don't *do* critical pedagogy, you *live* it, *how* just keeps creeping into the conversation. For example, when I told Dawn about self- and social transformation, emancipatory pedagogy, a spirit of inquiry, problem posing, she sighed and asked, "How?" When I told her to have students interview their parents, she queried, "Yeah but, what about the parents who question me because my students don't get dittos like the other kids?" When I told her to record her student-generated questions on the board, she came home and asked, "Okay, now I have 30 student-generated questions on the board, now what?"

The fact is that I love to play with the dialectic of *living* or *doing* critical pedagogy. The fact is that Dawn Wink is not as charmed with this as I am. So, for all the *Dawn Winks*, I hesitatingly offer these guidelines for *doing* critical pedagogy. I encourage you to take and shape them to fit the needs of your students. All the following guidelines are based on Paulo Freire's concept of problem posing:

> **to name**
> **to reflect critically**
> **to act**

The practitioners' voice in critical pedagogy must be as strong as the theorists' voice. It is always easier to state a theoretical concept than it is to live it with 30 to 150 students every day. The voice of critical pedagogy must flow in both directions. This ongoing dialogue with Dawn has offered me the opportunity to relearn and unlearn as her practice informs my theory and my theory informs her practice.

In the spirit of McLaren (1998), this is my attempt to pry theory away from the academics and incorporate it in educational practice (p. 167) as I have experienced it.

HISTORY HELPS: THREE PERSPECTIVES

History helps us understand why we do what we do. We are a reflection of all that has gone before us; we are indebted to the people and the ideas that have preceded us. When I started teaching in 1966, the world was a very different place. I do things very differently in my classes now, but I know that what I do in classes every day is touched by all the teaching, learning, and believing that has preceded me. Looking back historically can illuminate our present as we run to catch the future. In what follows, we will examine three approaches that represent unique educational beliefs and behaviors.

Transmission Model

The teacher is standing in front of the classroom, and the students are at their seats, which are in rows. They listen to what she says and write it down in their notebooks.

> *"A carrot is a root. We eat many roots. It is orange, and it is good for you. Other roots we eat are onions, beets, jicama, potatoes. Class, are you writing everything that I tell you? Today I will classify plants into those you can eat and those you can't. Make two columns on your paper and be sure to get every word I say for your homework. You will have a test on these exact words tomorrow. Who can name some other roots that we eat?"*

I suspect that every one of us has had a similar experience. Were you taught this way? Do you teach this way? Why? For centuries, the vision of the teacher in front of the class pouring knowledge into students' heads guided the image of pedagogy. In this instructional model, the teacher has the knowledge, and the students receive that knowledge. The teacher's job is to transmit knowledge. The teacher controls who knows what; power has always been a part of pedagogy.

I began my career in much the same way; I taught the way I was taught. In fact, I was a true 8-year-old direct instruction specialist, maybe even a zealot. I made my girlfriends sit on the basement steps, and; I stood on the cement floor below, and I taught. Oh, did I teach! I spoke; they listened. I had the knowledge in my head, and all I had to do was transmit it to them. What power. I could control their knowledge. For evaluation, they had to give it back to me exactly the way I gave it to them. Why in the world did they ever come to play with me? Fortunately, since the days of stair-step pedagogy, we have learned a lot about teaching and learning, not to mention the fact that the world has changed, too. Politically, economically, scientifically, ecologically, culturally, demographically, those days are gone. That was then; this is now.

Today, we have more complex understandings of who students are and how they learn. This new knowledge has raised questions about the traditional way of transmitting previous knowledge. Educators and researchers increasingly recognize the role students play in constructing knowledge and accessing new knowledge. The teacher-directed lesson too often lacks opportunities for students to interact with one another and with the ideas that they are studying. In addition, in linguistically diverse classrooms, the teacher-directed lesson is often incomprehensible to students who are still learning English. Students can't learn what they don't understand. Me, either.

To address these problems, more and more educators focus their pedagogy on discovery, exploration, and inquiry. Although intrigued by these ideas, many teachers find themselves at a loss in terms of how to structure these kinds of learning experiences in their crowded classrooms.

Generative Model

Now, imagine a classroom with small groups of students clustered around various learning centers. At each center students are exploring the properties of edible roots. One group is cutting a potato, a carrot, and an onion and dropping iodine on the pieces to see if they contain starch. Another group is sorting through an array of vegetables to determine which are edible roots. At still a third center, a group is setting up jars to sprout potatoes. The teacher moves around the room, quietly observes, and periodically interacts with various groups.

> *The teacher moves to the group that has jars for sprouting potatoes. "I see your group has used different amounts of water in your jars. Can you predict which potato will sprout first? Why?"*

The generative model maintains that students must actively engage in their learning process. In this model, students come together and construct or build their own knowledge. Learning is not passive. Students generate meaning as they integrate new ideas and previous knowledge. Simply put, students are participants in their own learning. The teacher's job is to structure and guide classroom experiences that will lead to student learning.

Transformative Model

Now, let's visit another classroom that is also studying carrots, and onions, and roots. The educational model being used in this classroom is historically rooted in the transmission and generative models. However, this model reflects, not only the changing world, but also our more complex understandings of meaningful teaching and learning. This model reflects today and prepares for tomorrow.

> *Imagine a classroom where small groups of students are outside working in their garden, which they planted several months ago. The students are digging the potatoes, carrots, and onions and weighing them. Based on their production costs, the students will determine their price per pound later in math class. The group has decided in their class meeting that they will sell a portion of the roots in order to*

earn money for the scholarships for a field trip. The remainder of the garden vegetables will be donated to the local food kitchen (Wink & Swanson, 1993).

In transformative pedagogy, or critical pedagogy, the goal includes generating knowledge and extends from the classroom to the community. Good constructive pedagogy often stays inside the classroom. Critical pedagogy starts in the classroom and goes out into the community to make life a little better. Some would say that this group of students is doing critical pedagogy.

Transmission to Transformative: An Example

Recently, I had an experience at the post secondary level with these three approaches: transmission, generative, and transformative. My goal was to share that immersion has many simultaneous and contradictory meanings often resulting in misinformation, disinformation (see Note 1), and harmful consequences for many language minority students. The public doesn't understand this. Many educators are confused about these multiple meanings, which result in very distinct programs and theoretical underpinnings.

> *This particular group of adult graduate students had already been working hard for several hours with me, so initially I explained that I had one more concept I wanted them to understand. It was important. If they were too tired, we would wait until the next day. No, they were ready, let's go.*

I am sure that some would describe this as an anticipatory set from the five-step lesson plan. Some would say that I was working to establish motivation. Maybe. However, I believe learning is about ownership. It is about making meaning together. It is about socially constructing knowledge. It is about experiencing. It is not about being talked at. If learning is not meaningful to students, it is irrelevant what the teacher does. Students have taught me this through the years. So did Dewey. So did Vygotsky. By the time I began the following lesson, the students owned their learning and were ready to experience a new idea.

Previously, I had made a chart to capture the three models of immersion and other dual language programs, as seen in Figure 4.1. I reflected on the various pedagogical approaches I could use.

First, I knew I could use the transmission model. It would be fast (for all of us) and efficient (for me). I could simply lecture on the information or give them the handout and tell them to read it. Then they could memorize

Program	Goals	Students	Teacher Preparation	Time
French Canadian Immersion	1.) English and another language (bilingualism/ biliteracy) 2.) High academic achievement	Language Majority Population	Credential	K–6
Structured English Immersion	English Only	Language Minority Population	English Only	9 Months
Bilingual, Dual, or Two-way Immersion	1.) English and another language (bilingualism/ biliteracy) 2.) High academic achievement 3.) Positive cross-cultural relations	Language Majority & Minority Populations	Credential	K–6
Maintenance/ Enrichment Bilingual Education	1.) English and another language (bilingualism/ biliteracy) 2.) High academic achievement 3.) Positive cross-cultural relations	Language Majority & Minority Populations	Credential	K–6
Transitional Bilingual Education	English Only	Language Minority Population	Credential or Paraprofessional Support	As fast as possible

FIGURE 4.1   Dual language models

what I had given them, and I could test them on the knowledge. I knew they would all get good grades on such a test, but I also knew that the information would not be meaningful and relevant. Nor would they remember it.

Second, I thought about a more interactive approach; I wanted the students to be socially constructing meaning as we worked our way through immersion. I wanted them to talk to each other; to ask questions; to slow me down. I decided to use a generative or constructive approach to sharing

Program	Goals	Students	Teacher Preparation	Time
French Canadian Immersion				
Structured English Immersion				
Bilingual, Dual, or Two-way Immersion				
Maintenance/ Enrichment Bilingual Education				
Transitional Bilingual Education				

FIGURE 4.2   Constructing the models

the information. I had a very large and very long piece of paper that covered the entire front of the wall. On this paper I had drawn the chart as seen in Figure 4.2; however, I drew only the framework of the chart.

I drew it all with a black marker. Under the program column, I wrote French Canadian immersion in red; bilingual (dual language) immersion in green; and structured immersion in blue. As immersion models were the focus of this lesson, I wrote the other program models in black. I did not fill in the information on goals, students, teacher preparation, or time for any of the program models. The empty spaces were waiting for us to generate or construct the knowledge together.

Of course, I was hoping that the class would also begin to generate other dual language models after they understood the three immersion models. First, I was interested to see if they would discover the parallels between dual language immersion and maintenance bilingual education. Second, I wanted to see if they would discover the difference between French Canadian immersion and dual language immersion.

Let the dialogue begin.

KWL

We began with a K/W/L approach. What did the students know **(K)**? What did they want **(W)** to know? How might they learn **(L)** it?

> K (know): The students talked in small groups about what they knew about immersion. They shared with the whole group. We recorded their prior knowledge on the chart and were able to fill in some of the blanks.
>
> W (want to know): They wanted to know about the empty blanks. They wanted the information about immersion that they couldn't generate together.
>
> L (learn): Usually students learn in various modes: from books, interviews, videos; on the Internet; at the library; from conversations with their families and friends; by collecting their own data, and so on.

Given the context (we had all been working very hard together for several hours, it was late, and I knew that I was exhausted), we decided that I would share the information with them, as I have experienced all three of these models. When we were finished, our chart reflected the following, as previously seen in Figure 4.1:

First: *French Canadian immersion* is a term used in the United States to refer to a program that serves language majority students. The goals are English and another language (bilingualism/biliteracy) and high academic achievement in 7 (K–6) years. The teachers are credentialed or certified bilingual or multilingual teachers. It has a long successful history in Canada.

Second: *Structured English immersion* (or as it is sometimes called in California, sheltered English immersion, structured English immersion, or even English immersion) is very different from the Canadian model. It is designed to serve language minority students. The goal is English dominance within 1 year. Teachers or paraprofessionals need not speak the language of the students, and the language of instruction is overwhelmingly in English (Krashen, Summer/Fall, 1998).

Although this model is programmatically and philosophically the exact opposite of the French Canadian model, the public often thinks they are the same. In addition, some politicians perpetuate this myth for their own political agenda, which happened in California in June 1998 with the passing of Proposition 227: English for the Children. The public was asked if they wanted their children to speak English. Of course, they did. However, if the proposition had been written differently, for example, do you want your children to speak English AND receive primary language support in content areas while learning English, perhaps the results would have been different, as is reflected in Krashen (1998, August) (see Note 3).

Other states are exploring comparable initiatives. For me, this seems to be a classic example of taking a very complex (social-cultural-pedagogical-linguistic-educational-political) issue and presenting it in a simplistic manner. It all reminds me of the old saying: For every complex issue, there is an answer that is obvious, simple, and wrong (see Note 3).

In my life I have noticed that voting on initiatives and propositions can be very confusing. Sometimes the wording leads me astray, and I have a hunch that someone is trying to fool me. In addition, I have noticed that sometimes the title of a proposition is the opposite of what it is really about. Because of this, I always vote absentee ballot so I can sit at home and think carefully. I don't want to be tricked or trapped. Because of my cautious nature, and because I care a lot about kids, and ideas, and words, I have developed the following rules:

Wink's Two Political Rules of Thumb.

Rule #1

Yes means no.

No means yes.

For example, Proposition 227 was named English for the Children. So, when I read that, I thought, Yes. And, when I think yes, that means I have to vote no. English for the Children: You bet. Of course, we all want English for the children.

Rule #2

Left means right.

Right means left.

I recently heard someone (whom I considered to be a right-wing person) say that his opponent (whom I considered to be a left-wing person) can't get left of him on this one. What?

All of this makes for interesting and lively family conversations, at least in our family. For example, I am a professor and a registered Democrat; my husband is a rancher and a registered Republican. We used to know the rules. We knew which were his issues and which were mine. And we sure knew left from right. Now it seems that we have all new rules to relearn and even unlearn. An old Chinese proverb is true for us today: We are blessed and cursed to be living in such interesting times. It is a new day. In fact, it is the turn of the century—time for all of us to find ideas that reflect our new world. Even ranchers and professors.

> **Third:** *Bilingual (dual or two-way) immersion* is designed to serve majority and minority students. The goals are English AND another language (bilingualism/biliteracy), high academic achievement, and positive intergroup relations in 7 (K-6) years. The teachers are credentialed or certified bilingual or multilingual.

Together the students had generated the knowledge on the three immersion programs, and they had gone beyond the immediate learning objectives to also generate their own knowledge regarding all dual language programs. When we finished, the graduate students/teachers in this group immediately pointed out to me that the bilingual immersion model is very similar to the French Canadian model, although it differs in one profound area: The bilingual immersion model is designed to provide biliteracy for *all* students, not just the majority language students, as is the French Canadian model. They also pointed out that the structured immersion model is essentially the old submersion model: sink or swim. We also discussed the fact that I could have handed them the copies of the completed chart (see Figure 4.1) and told them to read it. They were confident that the more generative/constructive way, although it took longer, was more effective. They felt they knew the materials.

Of course, I wish for this to be transformative learning for the students, but I can never control what students do with their own learning. Transformation requires that we shift from passive learners to active professionals and intellectuals in our own communities.

In summary, these three perspectives are not the only ways of teaching and learning. Of course, there are many ways of understanding complex processes like teaching and learning. I very much like Sonia Nieto's (1996; p. 319) advice to always keep the number 17 in mind as it reflects so well multiple perspectives on complex realities. Make no mistake about it: The interaction between teaching and learning, or pedagogy, is very complex. However, these three approaches (transmission, generative, and transformative) do provide a framework for us to reflect on our own pedagogy (see Note 4).

1. In the traditional classroom, instruction outcomes are often quite narrow and specific (memorized concepts, vocabulary, and skills); in the transformational model, student outcomes are as complex as the complexities of our diverse society. The problems students study and the range of possible solutions reflect the dilemmas of the larger society, and the complexity of society is mirrored in both the instructional strategies and content of classroom discourse.

2. The transformative lesson, or doing critical pedagogy, distinguishes itself in two ways from the generative, or constructive, lesson. First, it is designed so the students act upon and use their generated knowledge for self- and social transformation. The socially constructed knowledge of the classroom is to be applied in the social context of life. Second, this lesson design is inherently grounded in democratic principles.

3. The transformation model of education is another name for critical pedagogy. In this case the teacher and the students are not only doing critical pedagogy, they are living critical pedagogy. The fundamental belief that drives these classroom behaviors is that we must act; we must relate our teaching and learning to real life; we must connect our teaching and learning with our communities; we always try to learn and teach so that we grow and so that students' lives are improved, or for self-and social transformation.

TWO PERSPECTIVES

It is dangerous to reduce pedagogy to three perspectives. It is heresy to reduce it to two. I draw comfort from Jessamyn West, a Quaker writer, who believed that talent was helpful in writing, but guts were absolutely necessary. When we talk about putting the plural back in plurality, we certainly are not referring to 2, 3, or even 17. There are as many perspectives on pedagogy as there are committed, passionate souls who make their own road by walking (Horton & Freire, 1990). However, the previous three perspectives and the following two (Figure 4.3) are stereotypical experiences that we've all had with schools and communities. If a teacher has a transmission philosophy, the classroom practice might look like the column on the left in the figure. However, if the teacher has a more generative and/or transformational approach, the activity in the classroom might look more like the column on the right. It is often helpful to take time to reflect on our own theory and see how it turns into practice in our daily lives. Our beliefs (examined or unexamined) have a way of turning into behaviors that continually follow us around for all the world to see. If you are a teacher and

Theory	
Transmission Philosophy	Transformational Philosophy
Practice	
Teacher owns the knowledge.	Students and teacher own knowledge.
Students get knowledge from teacher.	Everyone knows something.
Start with text.	Start with students.
Purpose: students learn to memorize.	Purpose: students learn to learn.
Formal schooling has value.	Lifelong learning has value.
Schools control education.	Community controls schools.

FIGURE 4.3   Two ways of believing and behaving

haven't thought about this for awhile, just ask your students. They will know your theory because they are living your practice every day—even if you are unaware of it. Our theory informs our practice; our beliefs affect our behaviors in classes.

Making these two columns has been effective in getting teachers and learners to understand their own perspectives. Often teachers are so busy doing they don't take time to think about what they actually believe today and how they might turn those beliefs into behaviors in the classroom. Critical pedagogy calls upon us to examine and re-examine our beliefs about pedagogy.

One way to bring ourselves, as teachers and learners, to a place of reflecting on our own perspectives is to describe ourselves as learners: Do I prefer learning in a transmission approach? Or a more generative approach? Or a transformational approach? Do I always learn in the same way? Do the students in my classroom learn in the same way that I did? It goes without saying that no one way is right all the time for everyone—okay, I said it.

If you would like to try this with a group of teachers and learners, the following activity can be revealing and fun. First, ask the participants to describe a very powerful learning experience. Why was it effective? Second, ask the participants to write how they learn more effectively. Has it changed in the last 10 years? The last 20 years? Why? After writing, encourage everyone to share in small groups or pairs. To bring closure to the activity, draw a horizontal line across the full length of the chalk board (Figure 4.4). At one

Just tell me what you want me to learn.	Just get the heck out of my way.

(Students line up on the continuum of how they learn best.)

FIGURE 4.4   Where do you stand?

far end of this line, write: Just tell me what you want me to learn. At the other end of this long chalk line, write: Just get the heck out of my way. Next, invite the learners to come to the chalk board and line up along the continuum of perspectives so that they are standing at a point that represents their most effective learning style. Those who believe in the transmission model of education will undoubtedly line up near the statement Just tell me what you want me to learn. And I suspect that those with a more transformational approach will line up closer to other end of the chalk line, which represents a continuum of perspectives about pedagogy.

Just tell me what you want me to learn. Just get the heck out of my way (see Note 5).

Democratic Pedagogy

Democracy is at the heart of the transformative lesson. While schooling in the United States has historically prided itself on teaching democratic principles, how many schools are truly democratic? If you would like to explore this question, the next time you are with a group of teachers, initiate a discussion of democracy. It's all the rage. Everyone is for it. Then ask them if they work in a democratic school. I have done this on multiple occasions in large staff-development groups with many teachers. I consistently have been amazed at the level of cynicism of teachers when they discuss the lack of democracy in their own schools. It would take more than one hand for me to count the social studies teachers I know who teach democracy but admit they do not live and work in a democratic environment. Ah, these contradictions are confounding! It seems that in schools we teach it well; apparently, we don't live it quite as well.

> A society which makes provision for participation in its good of all its members on equal terms and which secures flexible readjustment of its institutions through interaction of the different forms of associated life is in so far democratic. Such a society must have a type of education which gives individuals a personal interest in social relationships and control, and the habits of mind which secure social changes without introducing disorder. (Dewey, 1944, p. 99)

The philosophy that supports transformative teaching and learning is founded on the principle that theory and practice are joined to form praxis. Not only must democracy be taught, it must be lived within the classroom, the school, and the community. Lesson designs that spring from this philosophical basis seek to break down the harmful forces of marginalization. This model of lesson design seeks to assure all communities of learners' equity and access to both academic resources and power structures of society.

The transformational activities that I am sharing in this chapter are all meant to be used in the classroom or with families in the community. I encourage you to adapt them to fit the context and the needs of the teachers and learners in your context (see Note 6).

Recently, I witnessed a marvelous example of democracy in action, although the word was never mentioned. This particular example focuses on democracy with teachers; however, the principles inherent in this vignette apply to all democratic actions—with students in the classroom or with families in the community.

Mark is a principal at a school that has a Latino American enrollment of 80 percent. At this school, as in many others, the "minority" is the "majority." If minority means less (in numbers), and majority means more (in numbers), I cannot say the Latino students are the minority at Mark's school. However, I have noticed that sometimes schools with a high enrollment of Latino Americans, African Americans, or Asian Americans are often called minority schools.

This always makes me wonder what minority now means. Could it be that minority means less and majority means more in hidden terms of value, status, prestige, power? Are we in schools unconsciously assigning value to one group of students and not another? As the world changes, our language must reflect these changes.

> *Mark and several teachers in the district had gone to an intensive workshop of labor relations sponsored by a nonprofit corporation that works to improve the relationship between districts and unions. Together the administrators and teachers had discussed the complex issues of consensus building, management styles, top-down and bottom-up administrative processes, and so on. The week Mark returned to his school, a regularly scheduled faculty meeting was planned.*
>
> *Traditionally, Mark had always prepared the agenda (mostly by himself) prior to the meetings. The established pattern was for Mark to speak and the teachers to listen. Teachers left their classrooms to immediately become passive learners. However, at this meeting, he and the teachers identified the topics that needed to be discussed, and together they created the agenda. Whereas previously the rules of the*

meetings were socially assumed based on protocol and imposed from the top down, now the teachers and administrators were jointly creating their own educational process. The emphasis had shifted from product to process.

In a separate discussion of democratic pedagogy relating to family involvement Dawn, my daughter, wanted to know "how-to-do-it." I reminded her of the various family and school activities she had experienced with me while she was growing up. It suddenly occurred to us that we were describing two very different approaches to school-sponsored family involvement. One approach is much more democratic. It seems that even when we do not see our beliefs, they tend to turn continually into visible behaviors that others can see, even if we don't. This happens even when we deny our beliefs. I am sure that both groups in Figure 4.5 think they are very democratic. However, the actual implementation of theory to practice tells a very different story.

Models for Parental Involvement

The We-Are-Going-To-Do-This-To-You Model of Parental Involvement
or
The We-Are-Going-To-Do-This-With-You Model of Parental Involvement

DOIN' IT TO 'EM	**DOIN' IT WITH 'EM**
Goal	
change the parents	change the schools
Objectives	
to melt into the pot	to melt the pot
to discuss building community	to build community
Characteristics of the Meetings	
teachers talk	teachers listen
families listen	families talk
families sit still	families interact
everyone leaves immediately after	people hang around
people leave space between them	people hug
kids go to a room with a sitter	kids work with families
teachers tell objectives	families tell stories
Result	
Dysfunctional School	Functional School

FIGURE 4.5   Models for parental involvement

The family graph activity in Figure 4.6 emerged when the graduate students in a class were creating oral histories. It is designed to demonstrate how much change has taken place in each person's life. It can be done in a class in an hour or it can be a month's activities of creating and chronicling a family history and making books. I have found that the participants usually are surprised to learn things about their historical roots that they have never known. All you have to do is to ask the participants to fill in the chart in the figure with their own history. After that, just get out of the way. This is student-centered learning.

MY FAMILY				
	My Grandparents	My Parents	Me	My Kids
School				
Work Career				
Religion				
Family				
Travel				
Politics				
Beliefs				
Daily Life				

FIGURE 4.6 Family graph activity

This new approach to teaching and learning challenges teachers to have complex pedagogical skills. The practices of teachers must be informed by new theories of unrestricted human development, inclusion, multiple voices, relationships, and everyone's everyday life (Garcia, 1993, p. 4). Traditionally, the teacher spoke, and the students listened. In the transformational model, teachers are challenged to expand the boundaries of classroom discourse. What the students say and feel matters. Discourse is based on equity and seeks to empower the voice of the most disenfranchised students. Teachers are called upon to understand that language is a powerful tool for the creation of knowledge and justice.

SO HOW DO YOU DO CRITICAL PEDAGOGY?

In transformative education, the spirit of inquiry leads the search for meaning. Students need to have classrooms in which they are safe to take risks. In this pedagogical model, teachers shift from control of knowledge to creation of processes whereby students take ownership of their learning and take risks to understand and apply their knowledge. Students and teachers come to realize that their actions can make a difference.

Problem Posing: Jonathan, An Example from the Community

How to do critical pedagogy? Let's reflect together on Jonathan. Why is it that I could learn so much about teaching and learning from him? Was I doing critical pedagogy? Problem posing is central in critical pedagogy; what does problem posing have to do with Jonathan?

Paulo Freire has taught that to teach and learn critically we can follow this straightforward guideline: *to name, to reflect critically, to act.* I have found this to be extremely effective in my own teaching and learning. However, I also have discovered that sometimes educators are doing/living this framework without realizing it. I also have discovered that when we ask teachers/learners *to name* the problem, they respond, "What?" Sometimes, I suspect that when I ask students *to name,* they think that I talk funny. When *we name* a problem, a situation, we are doing nothing more than conceptualizing critically and articulating clearly.

Let's rethink the experiences of Jonathan using this framework as a guide for our own reflection.

To name. In the Jonathan story, to name would be to say that he could not decode and encode; he could not read and write, as they have traditionally been defined. In this particular case, it is fairly easy to name. Sometimes, it is not so easy to name the problem.

To reflect critically. What did I do to reflect critically in this situation? I listened, I watched, I talked, I thought, I read, I called specialists, I tried lots of methods, I loved Jon. What did his parents do? All of this and more. In addition, they talked to the teacher (after teacher, after teacher), they listened to specialists, they went to student-study-team meetings, they agonized, they waited, they read and read and read stories to Jon, they provided other avenues of success, and they loved Jon. What did Jonathan do? He tried and tried and tried; and, periodically, he gave up and cried. How do I know all of this? I wrote and reflected and listened and read and wrote some more. For more than 6 years, the Jonathan files in my computer grew and grew. I had no idea what would happen with all of this.

To act. What did Jonathan's parents do? They enrolled Jon in a program that was expensive and very much the opposite of much of the advice they were receiving from many such as me, for example. I believe critical pedagogy helps us to grow in patience and courage. They had been patient long enough; now they needed to be courageous. What did I do to act? One week I sat down and opened the Jonathan files and pulled the story together because I saw that we can all learn from his experiences. In this particular case, I am not sure if I wrote the story or if it wrote itself.

During all of this time, did I ever think that I was doing critical pedagogy? Never. Not once. Was I doing critical pedagogy? Probably, but I prefer to think that I was simply living my beliefs. I care about Jonathan; I care about his entire family; I care about kids learning to read; I care about teaching and learning. I just had to keep a close eye on all of this. I couldn't stop myself. I suspect one has constantly and critically to reflect on learning, relearning, and unlearning. This is the hard part.

Now, here's the point: I believe that many educators are doing the very same thing in their own educational context. Every day with my work with teachers I observe similar powerful situations. Every night in my graduate classes, I hear incredible stories of teachers and students and families. At the grass roots level, teachers are making a difference in the lives of students, but I suggest that it is helpful to stop thinking of ourselves as just methodologists. We are more than that: Critical pedagogy enables us to understand that we also are professionals and intellectuals who have the power to take part actively in self and social transformation. Critical pedagogy makes us keep on keeping on.

Problem Posing: Miss Johnson, An Example from Secondary Schools

I have stated that all activities in this chapter are designed to be used in the classroom and/or the community. It is how and why we do activities that makes them critical. In the following vignette, we see how Miss Johnson turned her classroom into a community with critical activities. As this all took place many years ago, I am sure that Miss Johnson had never heard of critical pedagogy, but she was doing it.

Sometimes when we try to define problem posing it can be helpful to reflect on our own teaching and learning. I learned about Miss Johnson from Terry, a teacher and graduate student. Terry discovered the meaning of problem posing by thinking of her own experiences:

Problem posing always makes me think of liberation. If the purpose of education truly is human liberation, then why are we always trying to box in ideas? We are always trying to fit powerful ideas into a scope and sequence, a curriculum, a skill continuum, or another district-mandated process. Problem posing cannot be confined to these boxes. When I think of liberated people, I think of Maya Angelou who flies above all the boxes that others have created.

I think of my high school literature teacher, Miss Johnson. In her class, we lived problem posing every day, and we didn't even know it. She opened the world for us; she hated syllabi. Her enthusiasm ignited our journeys of learning. We had tons of books of all kinds in her class, and we had time to read whatever we chose. We read and talked and discussed and wrote, and we created a community in the process.

Miss Johnson listened to our hidden voices. She taught us to listen to each other. We learned that any problem can have many solutions.

> *She taught us to name; to reflect critically; and to act. I particularly remember one of the problems we posed.*

To name. This was during the sixties, and the girls were not allowed to wear pants to school. We were angry about this. We used to go to her room and talk about it. In her class, we knew we could name anything we wanted. We just didn't know that we were naming!

To reflect critically. We spent many lunch periods in her classroom talking about our anger. She would listen to each of us. If it mattered to us, it mattered to her.

To act. After considering several options, we devised a plan that was very radical in those days. We wrote letters and carried them to the student council, the administration, and the school board to ask that girls be allowed to wear pants to school. I remember the boys on the student council, the male administrators, and the men on the school board saying no: Girls had to wear dresses. However, the year after we graduated, pants were allowed for all students.

Apparently, I have overlooked a significant event in the histories of women of my age. On the same week that Terry wrote this reflection, another grad student/teacher handed in a splendid timeline that reflected the educational changes from Comenius to Freire. On this timeline she had written: 1966: *girls* finally were allowed to wear *pants* to school.

Principles of Problem Posing

> Teachers and Learners:
>
> trust each other;
> believe that their involvement will matter;
> understand resistance and institutional
> barriers to change;
> are aware of their own power and knowl-
> edge.

If we look back on Terry's experience, we can see that these principles of problem posing were embedded in this process. For example, the students and teacher trusted each other; they believed they could change the dress code; they knew the student council members, the administrators, and school board would probably say no initially; and they had a sense that they could make a difference because, after all, the dress code did affect their lives every day. It had very little effect on those who had created the rule. Perhaps perseverance should be another principle of problem posing.

The Teacher's Role in Problem Posing

> to create a safe place for it to happen;
> to ask hard questions for the students'
> musing;
> to assist students with codification.

Miss Johnson opened her classroom during lunch and after school. Terry and her friends knew they were welcome. As the girls talked, Miss Johnson periodically would ask questions that they had never considered. For example, who made this rule about pants? Miss Johnson had suggested to the girls that they write letters with their concerns; she had led them into the act of codification. As I have written previously, codification is the problem represented in some format. What might this codification look like? It can be captured in clay, in paint, in chalk, in pencil, in music, in any art form. In the process of problem posing, the learners capture their feelings and meanings about a problem.

Problem Posing: Stephanie, An Example from the Primary Grades

Stephanie listened as her students discussed their frustration with never being able to open their applesauce containers, which were served at lunch. The students consistently had to ask a teacher or an aide to open the containers for them. Instead of dismissing this topic as irrelevant because it was outside of the prescribed curriculum, Stephanie recognized the dynamic as one that mattered to students. As the students talked, Stephanie wrote their comments on the chalkboard. Stephanie allowed time for the students to articulate and conceptualize the problem. After the students had clearly named their problem, she asked them what could be done to alleviate this problem. The suggestions began as Stephanie continued to capture all the thoughts and language on the chalkboard. Finally, the group came to a consensus. They decided to write a class letter to the company. With the language on the board, the students were able to write independently to express their concerns. When we last called Stephanie, she reported the letters had been mailed, and they were awaiting a reply.

> *Doing critical pedagogy is grounded in some form of Freire's legacy of problem posing.*

In this case, Stephanie and the students recreated their socially generated knowledge to act upon one small condition of their own world. The transformative lesson design encourages students to act on their knowledge, and it seeks to create processes whereby students can see that their actions do count. Learning and teaching are integrated for self- and social transformation.

Problem Posing: Codification

Freeman and Freeman (1992) have clarified problem posing for many teachers whom I know, and they credit Wallerstein (1983) for expanding their understanding (See Note 7). Their codification model is grounded in the work of Freire and is amplified for teachers' ease in implementation. It has been my experience that many teachers are ready to problem pose; however, it is challenging, and they often are confused about codification. Freeman and Freeman offer the following model of codification:

- The code is a whole story, picture, or film.
- The code is based on the learners' lives.
- Learners identify and solve real-life problems.
- Learners work cooperatively to solve community problems.
- The goal is literacy for the learners.
- The goal is for teachers and students to empower themselves (Freeman and Freeman, 1992, p. 112).

Freeman and Freeman (1992) extend their codification processes to their version of problem posing in which they offer six phases. Adapting their model, I offer the following four phases of problem posing:

1. *Begin with the student's own experience.* In schools, we are so focused on doing, on covering, that we don't take time to think, to reflect, to muse. My sense is that we, as teachers, have failed our students by not taking the time to encourage students to reflect quietly on their lived experiences. Yes, learning can take place in noisy, interactive classrooms. Learning also can take place when we silently reflect. I have often heard Yetta Goodman, who teaches at the University of Arizona, say that the only thing teachers hate more than noise is silence. She is right.

2. *Identify, investigate, pose a problem within your own life.* At this point, teachers need to let go of control; student-centered learning is about to begin. Students generate knowledge about the problem; they brainstorm where, when, and how they can learn more about it. Students set out to learn what they want to know. They codify ideas; they interview experts in the community; they find information in the library, through technology, from any resource with accessible information. Teachers can facilitate this process by helping students find language to conceptualize and articulate their thoughts. Teachers ask leading questions about resources for more learning and possible connections to students' lives. Teachers stay out of the way.

3. *Solve the problem together.* After conceptualizing, articulating, and researching the problem, learners work together to solve the problem.
4. *Act.* Learners make a plan and act on it. Learners discover that their learning and their involvement really does matter. Learners are empowered by their own learning and action. They realize that their social interaction can lead to self- and social transformation.

Problem posing always ends with action. Once the learners have identified and captured (*named*) their concern, they take action, find solutions, and extend the dialogue of the classroom to the real world. What might this action look like? It can be writing a letter to the editor, governor, legislators, or presidents; interviewing others; capturing oral histories; meeting with policy-making committees; cleaning up a community; or beginning an environmental, social, cultural, or political action group.

Problem Posing: Reggie, an Example from Postsecondary

Reggie, a former drop-out and now a college freshman, was enrolled in a writing seminar. Although he was a bright student, every week in writers' workshop, Reggie sat. He rarely finished more than a paragraph.

> *To name.* Reggie would not write. Although he had returned to school, he was still angry and refusing to grow and learn and develop. His oppositional behaviors in the writers' workshop were holding back the further development of his own literacy. However, Reggie cared about his own writing and wanted to improve.

The instructor tried many different approaches to get Reggie to write. Nothing seemed to work. Finally, the instructor learned of a method referred to as *Voiced Writing* at a local university.

> *To reflect critically.* The instructor tried many different approaches; she discussed Reggie with her colleagues and local university professors. The instructor did not give up; she continued to reflect, not only on reasons why Reggie was not writing, but also how she might get him to want to improve his writing.

Finally, the instructor arranged for a tutor to come to writers' workshop to work alone with Reggie. The instructor helped Reggie understand the work that was necessary to pass the class, even as Reggie said that he did want to successfully finish the class. The tutor agreed to learn the method of voiced writing so that he could try it with Reggie.

To act: The instructor found a tutor and another method, voiced writing, to try with Reggie.

Ultimately, the human relationship between Reggie and the tutor is what brought about the transformation. The tutor discovered that Reggie could not write silently, but he could write if he spoke aloud as he wrote.

> *"Silence him, and he cannot write," the tutor told the instructor. After working with a partner and "talking" his own writing, Reggie discovered that he, indeed, could write. He only needed to talk as he wrote.*

There are many variations of voiced writing, but the process the instructor followed with Reggie follows:

- Reggie was paired with one other student, Lee.
- First, Reggie talked the writing assignment, while Lee wrote verbatim every word Reggie said.
- Second, Reggie read aloud what Lee had written.
- Third, Reggie and Lee exchanged roles. Lee talked the assignment, and Reggie wrote every word she said.
- Fourth, Lee read aloud what she had written.
- Finally, after Reggie and Lee had done this activity several times, they each returned to his and her own desk and continued to talk (quietly) and write their own words.

In other words, if you can talk, you can write. Just talk as you write.

As with all methods, how they are used and why they are used are basic in determining if the process will be effective with students, and as with all methods, there are as many variations as there are needs of students. In what follows I am sharing two other ways of approaching this activity.

The following activity might work well for students who are preparing for discrete point grammar tests. We teach grammar for 12 years in a row, and students still say, "I don't know grammar," which raises many disturbing questions about meaningful teaching and learning and types of assessment. However, this activity can demonstrate to them that they do know grammar; it's all in their head; they just have to talk it. Repeat the voiced writing activity, only have the pairs of students talk (and record) their oral responses on grammar exercises. Oftentimes, students will "talk" the isolated grammar exercises correctly. It demonstrates to the students that many do have correct grammar in their heads; they hear it on TV, the radio, and from teachers.

Students acquire a lot of correct grammar in this way and don't realize that they know it.

A second variation to use when confronted with students who say they can't write is to use this same paired activity and focus the "talk" to a description of the worst teacher they ever had. First, ask them to muse (think of sharp, mental images, visualize, feel the memory). Second, the "talk" student begins to brain dump—just saying all the images and words that are in her head; the writer records every word. Third, the "talk" student uses these words to talk about that teacher; the writer writes everything. The "talk" student reads to the writer what has been written, and they exchange roles. This activity of muse, brain dump, and write is much more powerful than it looks on paper, but students (of all ages) have to be walked through it the first few times. During the musing phase, the teacher must encourage the students to think in pictures and sense, to visualize every aspect. During the brain-dumping phases, students just take the visual images and use words to describe them. During the writing phase, the students use their own language to generate their own cognition. Good problem posing always revolves around concepts that the learners care deeply about or have experienced.

In summary, problem posing takes place when people begin with a spirit of inquiry and questioning of situations that directly affects their own lives. Problem posing ends with actions and transformations in their lives and in their context. Problem posing begins again.

Here is the secret: If you do critical pedagogy, you will be problem posing. To problem pose is (a) to name, (b) to critically reflect, (c) to act. There you have it: how to do critical pedagogy.

THE ESSENCE IS IN THE EXPERIENCE

> A primary responsibility of educators is that they not only be aware of the general principle of the shaping of actual experience by environing conditions, but that they also recognize in the concrete what surroundings are conducive to having experiences that lead to growth. Above all, they should know how to utilize the surroundings, physical and social, that exist so as to extract from them all that they have to contribute to building up experiences that are worth while. (Dewey, 1947, p. 35)

In what follows are activities in direct response to the readers of the first edition who asked, How do you do it? My final cautionary word on methods: You have to experience them. Dewey was right. Reading about methods is a poor second. Please take these methods and adapt to your context; to the needs of the students; to your own unique pedagogical gifts. If you are anything like me, new methods often do not work well the first time. It takes experience to understand how to turn methods into critically reflective actions within communities.

Easy Method/Difficult Text

The following new activities are not new per se. However, one of my most interesting relearning experiences since the publication of the first edition is that many activities can become vehicles for critical reflection and action depending on why and how they are used. I know. I should have known. However, it was yet another relearning experience for me when I wanted to introduce some rigorous ideas to a group of international educators during a fast-paced summer school session. Here is how I now remember what I relearned with this marvelous group of educators.

The more critical the text, the easier the method. I wanted the students to read Pennycook (1994), to understand and internalize the ideas, and hopefully to return to their various homelands around the world and continue to reflect and, perhaps, even to act on their learning. I considered many options before deciding how to access the text. Finally, I decided to use activities that are relatively easy and ones I knew well. Walking to class that day, enjoying the beach air of Palma, Mallorca, Spain, I worried that the students might be insulted or demeaned by my selection of easy methods. The exact opposite happened. The easy methods became an effective way of accessing rigorous content.

The students were adults who teach English all over the world; in other words, they were English as International Language (EIL) teachers. Pennycook's objective in *The Cultural Politics of English as an International Language* is to encourage international teachers to think in new ways about the teaching of English. He weaves the cultural and political implications of the spread of English throughout the pages of his text. He suggests that EIL teachers are gatekeepers of knowledge, even though they may never have critically reflected on their unexamined role in the process. His reference section is complete with the various international scholars who support the idea that teaching English internationally is often not far afield of the socio-cultural, political, historical, and economic context. His thesis is a critical challenge to many dominant ways of thought.

Pennycook says that we come from a history that teaches that English is natural, neutral, and beneficial. To this traditional pattern of thought, he offers a second perspective as he documents the various ways in which the spread of English has often been quite deliberate. He writes about the worldliness of English. He assumes that a language (English, in this case) is not just A language, but rather it is an inherent and complex part of cultural perspectives. Language does not exist in a vacuum; it is not neutral. The worldliness of English assumes the plurality of perspectives; it is not monological. Language is in constant change, and meanings are always being created, adapted, and changed. In essence, Pennycook deconstructs the assumptions of many well-intentioned teachers who go abroad to teach English—the very teachers I was now teaching (see Note 8).

As I assigned Pennycook, I was quite sure that this would be a new idea for this group of teachers. My initial sense was that they had come from a traditional pattern of thought. I was quite sure that there would be resistance, anger, and denial.

As I reviewed the ideas of Pennycook, I considered the various approaches we could use for teaching and learning. I knew the transmission model (me talking and students listening) would never work. I was sure that I had to do something interactive so the students could play with the ideas. I also wanted something transformative to come from this experience. I was hoping that the students would critically reflect on their own roles in teaching English in an international context when they returned home. However, I am well aware that I cannot control the future. If Pennycook's ideas were to become transformative in the lives of these students/teachers, it was really up to them. If the generative knowledge that we constructed together was ever to be transformative in their various contexts around the world, I suspected that I would never know it. I believe that we can only critically, reflectively, interactively, and actively approach our own pedagogy and hope that students will do the same.

I somewhat nervously approached our 6-hour class on the day that we were to discuss Pennycook (1994). With our very tight schedule, I knew that we could only devote a day or two for this text. The students approached class tired and angry: frustrated and fearing that (a) they did not understand the text, and/or (b) they understood only too well. Contradictions are a common experience among critical educators. We began the following easy methods to access difficult text. The results were surprising. In fact, the exact opposite of what I feared happened. This certainly isn't the only time that I have marveled at the contradictions in pedagogy while doing critical pedagogy. As we worked through the ideas of the worldliness of English, I relearned methods, and the students unlearned some of their long-held, but previously unexamined, assumptions about teaching English internationally. I have since tried this in other contexts with similar results, but my descriptions of the next four methods will revolve around only this international context.

POPCORN

How-to-Do-It

- Students choose a small section from the text that they liked or didn't like.
- When each student has chosen, one student stands and reads her passage. Other students listen. No comments or questions until each student has shared individually.
- The first student calls a second student to stand and read. When all are finished with their individual readings, students are encouraged to share with the whole group (or in small groups) their reactions to the readings.

The Experience

First, I can vividly recall the look of relief on their faces as they realized that I was not going to call on them or talk at them. It took this group of 20 adult students about 20 minutes to choose their individual passage. It took the whole group about 30 minutes to slowly read their challenging readings. The ideas were complex, new, and threatening. There were great periods of time when everyone sat and thought about the passage before moving to the next reader. If you had walked by our classroom, it would have looked as if we weren't doing anything. We were reflecting critically; we were thinking deeply. After the individual readings and the following dialogue, Fiona, an adult student who teaches in Palestine, wrote

> *It forced us to look deeply at text and decide what hit each of us most. It triggered profound, and often hidden, thoughts about why we felt one way or the other.*

Incidentally, I have done the Popcorn activity on numerous occasions with the first edition of this book; it is always lively, fun, and enlightening. I am constantly amazed at how much I have learned with this method.

PAIR SHARE

How-to-Do-It

> - Pair students; each individual within a pair then chooses and explains a specific portion of the text.
> - Questions are asked and discussed within pairs.
> - After pair sharing, pairs share their discoveries and reflections with the whole group.

The Experience

Again, I remember the relief on their faces when, for the second time, they realized that they would not have to answer questions in front of the whole group and/or to be embarrassed by their lack of understanding or frustration. This text is challenging for many good readers, particularly on the first reading. I could sense the group warming to Pennycook's ideas because they had control of the learning. Again, Fiona wrote in her ethnography of the class:

> *We discovered what was meaningful and relevant to each of us. Spontaneously, we began to compare and contrast with our peers' perceptions. Eventually, we created a comparison and contrast chart on the board. Our ideas were so diverse. By the end of this activity, we moved from a personal interpretation to a discussion of why we had our interpretation.*

The dialogue deepened in ways that I could never have triggered if I had presented the material in a transmission model of pedagogy. The students began to make meaning of the ideas, instead of blaming me for ideas they found challenging.

DIALOGUE JOURNAL

How-to-Do-It

> - Students choose any portion of the text and read it silently.
> - Students write privately in their journals their reactions to the passage.
> - Each student shares the passage from the text and her written reflections with another.

In small groups or whole group activities, I believe there has to be an understanding that students can choose not to share. They simply need to say, "I pass."

The Experience

Fiona wrote the following in her class ethnography:

> *We enjoyed the quiet, reflective time to think and write. We discovered that we liked accessing the text on our own terms. And, we particularly valued sharing our private reactions with only one other person.*

BLOOM'S TAXONOMIES
How-to-Do-It

- Choose a specific and demanding piece of text prior to the activity.
- Assign and read it in class silently.
- Divide the whole group into 6 smaller groups, each representing one of Bloom's levels of taxonomies.
- Assign each small group to relate their assigned level of taxonomy to the reading assignment.

The Experience

First, none of the students could remember all six levels. Can you name them right now? We had a good laugh about this and decided we needed to shift into a truly generative mode of learning. It was coffee-break time, and we assigned ourselves the task of generating the six taxonomies with our colleagues. When we came back to class, each of us was able to recite all six taxonomies: knowledge, comprehension, application, analysis, synthesis, evaluation. This may have taught more about generative, constructive, interactive teaching and learning than anything I could have done.

Each small taxonomy group shared with the whole group. For example, the knowledge group shared their knowledge; the comprehension group, their comprehension; the application group explained how they could apply their learning; etc. It became a process of students realizing that they had grown quite familiar with Pennycook's ideas, which had seemed so abstract, esoteric, and even infuriating only a few hours ear-lier.

As I reflect on my hesitation to share Pennycook with this group of EIL teachers, I am now aware of how much they were affected by his message and our approach to accessing his message. Although we read several other demanding texts during this summer school session, none hit as close to home as Pennycook. Nothing related more to their lives. These easy methods made the students reflect critically on the use of English in the international context, but also on the unexamined role they might be playing in this process.

TEACHING AND LEARNING ON THE DESERT

In what follows, I will share other methods that I have used in various places. The stories that follow are all taken from a teaching/learning experience I had with a group of grad students/teachers in Arizona.

FOUR CORNERS

This activity works well in all areas of curriculum, negotiating meaning of text, previewing, reviewing, and/or summarizing a body of knowledge. The activity can be used to generate questions from the students or to answer questions that the instructor wants to emphasize. Later, I will demonstrate that it is also effective for bringing in student voice.

How-to-Do-It

- Tape a large piece of butcher paper to the wall at each of the four corners of the room.
- Each piece of paper can be blank for student-generated questions that they need to be studied, or the instructor can write a specific question on each of the four pieces of paper.
- Divide the whole group into four smaller groups; each group needs one colored marker, and each group uses only its one color, which is different from the other groups.
- After each small group has discussed how it will answer each question (or which question it would like to generate for the whole group), the smaller groups rotate to each paper writing their answers (or questions). After the groups have rotated and answered their questions, the whole group can analyze and discuss the answers.

The Experience

We have often heard that we, as teachers, need to bring in student voice (Poplin & Weeres, 1992). But how? This method works well with a little adaptation. Oftentimes, we are in a situation in which we know the students have intense feelings about, or it is something very meaningful to them. Maybe it is a social event at school or in the community; maybe it is an act of injustice they are feeling; maybe it is confusion about assignments; maybe it is our syllabus. Or maybe it is our teaching. We all have had these experiences and will again. We come from a tradition that assumes that when these difficult teaching/learning (pedagogical) moments arise, we should take more control: Make the students sit down; make the students be quiet; make the students do a required assignment. Sometimes, we (or, at least, I) have shifted to the old transmission model of teaching to gain control: teachers talk; students listen. I may have even reverted to teaching harder, not better. The next time you want to bring in student voice, I suggest you try this.

> *In Arizona, the graduate class was scheduled only on two, very long, 3-day weekends during the semester with various assignments due during the semester. Anyone who has ever taught or learned in class for 5 hours on Friday night, 8 hours on Saturday, and 8 hours on Sunday knows that this can be exhausting, particularly when all the students are also full-time teachers, and the vast majority are parents, too. These are people with demanding and complex lives. Without weekly meetings during a semester, it is easy for misunderstandings and confusion to emerge. Therefore, when I returned for the second intense weekend, I wanted to be sure that all student concerns were taken care of at the beginning of our session. However, because I was so far away geographically from the students, I didn't know what the issues might be. I needed to bring in student voice.*

For the first round of the 4-corners' activity, I chose four questions to write on the large pieces of paper.

1. Which assignment is most frustrating at this moment and what should we do about it?
2. What is the most important thing your group learned during our last weekend together?
3. What is the most important thing you have learned since we have been apart?
4. What can I (the professor) do to assist you with your learning, and what can you (the student) do?

When we did this activity in class, the small groups were animated as they discussed the processes of the class, the assignments, their questions. After each group had answered each of the questions at the four corners, the colored markers made it evident to all of us the unique concerns of each small group. I was surprised when the students expressed repeated concern about a particular assignment. It was clear that they did not understand my expectations and that they needed more in-class time working on this major activity. Together we juggled our schedule for the next 8-hour day to include time for this. Although this activity took an hour of our valuable time together, when student voice was heard and respected, students were much more ready to hear teacher voice.

THE MESSENGER AND THE SCRIBE
How-to-Do-It

- Prior to the activity, the instructor chooses one piece of text.

- Make copies of the text and tape in multiple places on the walls of the classroom.

- Place the students in pairs; one is the messenger, one is the scribe.

- When the activity begins, all who are messengers run to the wall, read the text, return to the scribe, and repeat the text exactly. The scribe writes exactly what the messenger says.

- Throughout the activity, the instructor can change the roles of the scribes and messengers.

- The instructor needs to stay out of the way. This is lively and fun whether 5-year-olds, 15-year-olds, or 55-year-olds are doing it.

- When one pair finishes, the activity stops while this pair reads exactly what is written on their paper. If there are any errors, the activity begins again.

- Obviously, this activity works well for listening, for spelling, for grammar, and punctuation (see Note 9).

The Experience

When we did this activity in Arizona, I was not interested in listening, spelling, grammar, or punctuation. I was interested in content. I was interested in an idea. I wanted the group to begin a discussion of parental involvement, so I chose Models for Parental Involvement (Figure 4.5). In this case we placed the copies of text out in the hall, as it was a long Saturday, and the building was empty except for us. This made the activity more fun and more challenging. When we finished, the students (adults) discussed ways they could adapt this activity to their own context and then slowly began to discuss their various experiences with family involvement in their own community. By the end of the discussion, they were acknowledging the important role they play in improving the quality of parental involvement at their school sites.

COMPREHENDING/COMPREHENSION

I learned this activity from Cecilia, a young woman who teaches in Saudi Arabia. However, there are parts of this activity that remind me of one I learned from Farr and Tone, (1994) several years ago. I suspect that this method has been adapted and adopted several times. I encourage teachers to use their knowledge to shape any method to fit the needs of the students.

Comprehending is a process; comprehension is a product. Good readers think about their reading while they are reading; good readers share their thoughts about reading; and good readers write about their reading. Most good readers go through this process of comprehending unconsciously. It is helpful to teach beginning readers some of the comprehending processes that good readers do automatically. The purpose of this activity is to help readers learn (a) to predict and to share orally their thoughts; (b) to connect new knowledge with prior knowledge as they privately write their thoughts, and (c) to use any context clues in the text or any other thoughts that pop into their head while reading. It is the teacher's responsibility to pre-read the material and to make decisions about where in the text the readers will be asked to stop reading.

How-to-Do-It

> - Students are paired or placed in small groups. Each reader will also need a private journal or blank paper.
> - The instructor decides on the three stopping places in the text prior to the activity.
> - First, students read until the first predetermined stopping place in the text. In pairs, the students orally predict with their partner.
> - Second, students read until the next stopping place. At this point each reader connects their new knowledge with prior knowledge as they write privately in their journals. Each reader shares with partner what they have written—if they choose to do so.
> - Third, everyone reads until the last stopping place in the text. At this point, in pairs the readers share their meaning making from context clues or any other thoughts that popped into their heads.

The Experience

My purpose for doing this with the teachers in Arizona was twofold. First, I wanted them to have an opportunity to experience various methods; and second, I wanted to prepare the students for the problem posing that was to follow. Once again I was using a method simply as a way of accessing text. For this purpose, I chose Two Ways of Believing and Behaving (see Figure 4.3), because I wanted students to think about their theoretical grounding.

Prediction is the first phase of the activity, and I was hoping that students in small, safe groups would predict some of their future actions based on their individual belief structure.

Writing is the second phase of this activity, and I had chosen The Mess, printed at the end of this chapter, because I wanted the students to write (and thus to think) about problem posing. The Mess is simply another way of problem posing (See Figures 4.7 and 4.8). As they shared their writing with their colleagues, I knew they would hear differing perspectives, and their understandings would grow.

Talking about context clues or anything else that popped into their heads is the final phase of this activity. As the students talked about other context clues and other things popped into their heads, I remember hearing them say that they wanted to enter into problem posing. And so we did.

PROBLEM POSING ACTIVITY: LITERACY

The archetypal way of doing critical pedagogy is to experience problem posing: *to name, to reflect critically, to act.* And, then begin again. When you have long since lost this book, I hope you will remember one of the greatest legacies of Paulo Freire: problem posing. I have purposely saved this specific example to place here as a lead in to the final activity of this chapter so that you will see that problem posing need not be only a three-step process. If you choose to problem pose in 3, 5, or even 17 steps, it doesn't matter as long naming, reflecting critically, and acting are inherently a part of the transformative process.

How-to-Do-It

> • *to name:* Form small groups and ask each person to name (state) a problem in her school site. After each has named a problem (or contradiction, or conundrum, or sticky situation, or mess), the small group builds consensus and chooses one problem to name.
> • *to reflect critically:* Each small group reflects critically and searches for various approaches to improve the situation.
> • *to act:* The small group lists a recommended action to be taken.

The Experience

This experience took place in Arizona with the same group of teachers as in the previous example. You will recall that they had already read about The Mess (see Figures 4.7 and 4.8) as part of their reading assignment for the activity Comprehending and Comprehension. At this point in our relationship, I think that they knew about problem posing; they knew about The Mess. I think they assumed that problem posing had to be only this prescribed three-step process. I wanted them to see that it could be three steps, or four, or however they organized it. I also wanted them to know that it is cyclical and can be experienced in multiple ways. More than anything, I wanted them to experience problem posing.

To Name

In this context, the problems named were the many mandated tests; lack of youth activities; the media; lack of unity and articulation among local school districts; lack of parental involvement; the high social value placed on monolingualism; a lack of literacy events locally; and low teacher salaries.

We listed everything on the large blank pieces of paper taped to the wall. Next, the students read the list and reflected privately with their colleagues. Our challenge was to chose one situation as a whole group to continue the activity. We began by eliminating some of the problems posed. After much discussion, the group chose to focus on literacy within the community, including students, families, and educators.

To Reflect Critically

Next, we began the process of reflecting and naming possible approaches to solutions. I encouraged the teachers to think creatively. They had just read about The Mess, so they knew there were to be no boundaries on our thinking. We were searching for options to improve literacy and increase literacy events throughout the community.

The following possible approaches were listed on large pieces of paper taped to the wall: support local libraries, buy books for schools; create mentoring processes, outreach to senior citizens to encourage their participation in literacy activities, fund a bookmobile, create reading buddies with older and younger students, and create scholarships. Throughout this process, our codes were as simple as filling in the large blank sheets of papers with the students' thoughts.

To Act

Critical pedagogy calls us to action. Critical pedagogy is good interactive pedagogy that extends to the real world, to the local community. The teachers knew we were heading for action. Because we had just read about The Mess, we chose to follow that action process and make true individual commitment statements, which were then taped to the wall. The students' individual commitment statement follow.

I commit to

- Get more books for my classes.
- Bring in people to read to my class.
- Allow choice for my students' reading.
- Bring more family members into my classroom.
- Donate books to the local library on my birthday and family members' birthdays.
- Take time for reading.
- Bring in scientists to my science classes.
- Clean out my boxes of old comic books and bring them in for the students to read (see Note 10).
- Donate money to the local library.
- Share my own books with the students in my classes.
- Create fund-raising activities.
- Develop an award system in class to encourage reading.
- Make reading fun.
- Work with the parents of my students on all of the bureaucratic forms they need to know how to complete.
- Provide information for families about what they can do at home with their children to improve their literacy levels.
- Discuss library issues with the staff at my school site.
- Educate myself more about literacy.

Now, what has happened since then? How have those commitment statements become action? As with all transformative actions, it all depends on the teachers and learners who are involved. Just as with the international students who read about Pennycook, I may never know what happens with literacy and the commitment statements in this community on the desert. In the Preface/Introduction of this book, I likened our work to that of farmers: We plant seeds. How they grow and develop depends on many other factors in the environment. At the time of this writing, I know that this list of commitment statements still hangs on the walls of this university classroom; the ideas have been sent to a state professional newsletter; and the commitment statements have been published in the local paper for all to see. Freeman and Freeman (1992; 1994; 1998) often write that one of the most effective principles of pedagogy is to have faith in the learners. To be honest, I have complete faith that good things will develop around this group of committed grad students/teachers.

A MESS

I have saved the best activity for last. I encourage you to adapt this and try it. Make it work for you. There are surprises every time you enter into this type of process.

First, you start with a mess (Figure 4.7). In this case, a mess is any situa-

---

First, You Start with a Mess

Start with a mess (problem, contradiction, difficult situation). Define it. Name it.

Learn more about it.
How can we learn more about this?
Who knows what about this?
How will we share information with the group?

Alternative approaches.
List all of the ideas that might work. Think wildly and passionately.
Dream. Think up utopias.
Collectively, choose an approach.

Preparation.
What are the roadblocks? How can we prepare for them? What new problems might this approach create? What are possible solutions for these new problems? What could go wrong? What role might others play if we decide to try to change this?

Action plan and evaluation.
Create a timeline and plan of action.
Do it; fix it. Do it; fix it.

Write a commitment statement.
We commit to . . .
I commit to . . .
Members of the group share personal commitment statements and agree to use their own expertise to help fix the mess.

Begin again.
Redefine and rename the new mess.

FIGURE 4.7   First, you start with a mess

tion within an educational space that needs attention. It is something that is not working for someone.

I adapted this framework from Lieberman (1986) and García (1993). Tove Skutnabb-Kangas also has influenced this model; she immediately thought of the mess as creative chaos. I have been experimenting with various groups with this particular process, and so far, it is has been extremely powerful for all involved. In each case, we needed a minimum of 3 hours walking though the process. We worked in small groups at each phase and shared with the whole group after each phase. The commitment statement (the last step, which is really the first) is fundamental to the cyclical process. When you finish, each participant will have made a commitment to change, and each participant will leave with new questions. In all fairness, I must mention that this process does not lead to smaller messes; it leads to more critical questions.

Before beginning the steps of this process, the facilitator and the participants need to generate a list of messes. What are the problems? Concerns? Questions? The facilitator captures all the ideas and records them for all to see. The facilitator begins by asking each member of the whole group to reflect privately before joining a smaller group. After this, the facilitator again records more questions from the group. Next, the participants are encouraged to sit in small groups by messes. Those who are interested in a particular question can problem pose as a small group. Once in the small group, the facilitator asks that each member individually share her concern with the group. Once this has happened, each small group is given the following format to guide their discussion:

At times, I have streamlined the process into the following steps (Figure 4.8). Depending on the participants and the amount of time available to you, try it in the following manner:

This is not a one-shot activity; rather, it is the beginning of more critical teaching and learning with colleagues. The commitment statements that end

---

Find a mess.
Learn more about it.
What could be some alternative approaches?
Action plan and evaluation.
Write a commitment statement.
Name a new mess.

FIGURE **4.8** Find a mess; fix a mess

the activity provide authentic experiences in which teachers and learners discover their own power.

What works? We all want to know (Figure 4.9). I am sure that the answers will vary for each of us. I have tried to summarize what has worked for me in my experiences in schools (see Note 11).

Recently, a teacher suddenly raised his hand and told me that you can't really do critical pedagogy; it is more a state of mind. I agree. It calls on us to see and to know in new critical ways. It calls upon us to reexamine our own as-

---

So, What Works?

Taking time.
Tossing the texts.
Asking: but why?
Reflecting.
Conceptualizing and articulating our own philosophical
assumptions.
Understanding why and how beliefs change.
Naming the power structures: critically reflecting and acting
on them.
Relearning and unlearning.
Acknowledging the powerful emotions of power, racism,
classism, sexism.
Understanding and being able to articulate the new
global realities.
Challenging our long-held assumptions about teaching
and learning.
Reading hard books.
Entering into dialogue.
Recognizing the contradictions in our own lives.
Recognizing our own power, expertise, knowledge, and role.
Seeing with new eyes.
Taking time and creating a safe place.

FIGURE 4.9   What works

sumptions. We don't do critical pedagogy; we live it. We are challenged to live our beliefs. Each of us has a set of beliefs about values and education. These beliefs come to life every day in our behaviors in the classroom. What is it that each of us believes? Why do we believe this? Have our beliefs changed? An examination of our own beliefs and accompanying behaviors can lead each of us to rethink our approach to teaching and learning in our own classrooms.

> *"If you watch a teacher long enough, you will know her beliefs. I call this the Belief Indicator," Gary said to his classmates in the teaching credential program.*
> *"The what?" his classmates said in unison.*
> *"The Belief Indicator," he said. "Just watch your professors; they all have one. What they do every day in class tells you all about their beliefs. It always reminds me of the old adage, The eyes are the window to the soul. I think the methods are the windows to a teacher's philosophy."*

Obviously, Gary understands my thesis. Just as Gary told his classmates, our behaviors are a reflection of our beliefs; our practice reflects our theory.

The purpose of transformative education is to create processes whereby students can see that their actions do count. They are encouraged to take the learning from the classroom and to engage locally and socially. This model of learning and teaching assumes that the generation of knowledge in the classroom leads to the betterment of life for the student or for the community. Knowledge is created to influence their world; it is no longer a passive ingredient designed only for the classroom.

I ask one central question: Why do we do what we do? In the spirit of reflective teaching and learning, in the spirit of attempting to learn how to do critical pedagogy, I challenge you, the readers, to reflect critically on your own philosophy and how it is reflected in your practice. There is no one best way to do critical pedagogy, but all ways involve critical reflection by teachers and learners together.

LOOKING AHEAD FOR ELUSIVE METHODS

How Do You Think You Do Critical Pedagogy?

NOTES

1. Although the word, *disinformation,* is used in many other contexts, it is also used to refer to false information that is spread (knowingly or unknowingly) by opponents of bilingual education. For more on how this happens, I refer you to Cummins (1996), Chapter 8, *Disinformation in the Information Age: The Academic Critics of Bilingual Education.* This book is available through California Association of Bilingual Education, 660 S. Figueroa Street, Suite 1040, Los Angeles, CA 90017 (www.bilingualeducation.org). For more about the deliberate misrepresentation of education and language, see Goodman (1998) and Taylor (1998). All three of these books may push you into that uncomfortable unlearning zone, and therefore, are important to be read.

2. Krashen (Summer/Fall, 1998). This source, which is published by TESOL (http://www.tesol.edu/) is a very short review of the literature that overwhelmingly demonstrates that children do not acquire enough English in 1 year to do grade level work in mainstream classrooms. Another way to answer this question is simply to reflect on how long it has taken you, or would take you—even with your high level of literacy and rich academic experiences.

   Structured immersion is a programmatic model that has rarely been used, except in isolated cases. However, many classrooms are de facto English immersion for the majority of language minority students with disastrous consequences for these students. For those who are in favor of English-only initiatives in schools, it is already the reality for most language minority students. The educational and social consequences have had a profound negative effect for the students directly involved and for all of us who care about schools. For more on this read August and Hakuta (1997). Flood, Lapp, Tinajero, and Hurley (December 1996/January, 1997) provide another concise overview of the debate swirling around immersion.

3. Krashen (August, 1998) asks "Why did California voters pass Prop 227? They thought they were voting for English." This question, often referred to as The Crawford Question, demonstrates that, contrary to popular opinion, California voters do support primary language support for students in the process of acquiring English (Krashen, 1999a). The Los Angeles Times (April 13, 1998) poll shows that 63% voted for Prop 227 because they believed they were voting for English; only 9% polled felt that bilingual education was not effective. In the same poll, 32% were in favor of English-only and over 60% supported the idea of using the first language as support for learning. The Dallas News (June 28, 1998) produced nearly identical results. A third poll was conducted by Steve Krashen and James Crawford in the LA area, and it supported the find-

ings of the LA Times and the Dallas News and further demonstrated that few people knew what was in Prop 227, and if they had known, 71% would have voted against it. Unfortunately, much misinformation and disinformation were made available to the voters. McQuillan (1998a) looks at the early data on student achievement since the passage of the English-only mandate.

4. Others have used different language to describe these three approaches to teaching and learning. Of course, there really are more than these three approaches; it is a continuum of transmission to transformation. For further reading, I encourage you to see Freeman and Freeman (1994). In this book, they adapt the language of Lindfors (1982) and describe these three approaches as student as plant, builder, and explorer. The student as plant relates to the transmission model of education in that the teacher provides the students with all that the student needs. The idea of the student as builder reflects the constructive and generative approaches to knowledge and literacy. The student as explorer moves on the continuum towards transformational teaching and learning. Rethinking Schools (1995) also explores these various approaches to teaching and learning (see Note 5, chapter 3). Cummins (1996) describes these three somewhat typical approaches to teaching and learning: traditional, progressive, and transformative.

5. This activity, which revolves around a line representing the continuum of pedagogy from transmission to transformation, was shared with me by Sharon Whitehead, a public school teacher and doctoral student. She learned it in a seminar conducted by Mark and Maxine Rossman of The Graduate School of America of Minneapolis, Minnesota (December 1998).

6. For further reading on family involvement, I encourage you to explore the idea of Funds of Knowledge, as generated by Luis Moll (1990). This idea has recently been adapted and expanded by Patterson et al. (1998).

7. Wallerstein (1983) contains very specific and diverse examples of problem posing with students in the process of acquiring English.

8. If you wish to read more about the group of international scholars who deconstruct the idea that the spread of English is natural, neutral, and beneficial, I suggest that you go to the library and explore almost anything published by J. Fishman, R. Phillipson, T. Skutnabb-Kangas, J. Naysmith, D. Pattanayak, J. Tollefson. This list is not all-inclusive; you will find more to read in the bibliographies of these scholars. For further reading of the power of language on the North American continent, see Crawford (1999) or his Language Policy Website at http://ourworld.compuserve.com/homepages/jcrawford/

9. While experiencing Messenger and the Scribe with this group of teachers/students, I learned from Natalie Hess, a professor at Northern Arizona University, Yuma, that the inventor of this activity was originally Mario Rinvolucri, who called it, The Messenger Dictation. It is a pleasure to cite him, as he is known to be generous in his acknowledgements of his colleagues. I also thank Natalie Hess, who enriched all of us in this intense class with her knowledge, her pedagogy, her personal library, and her commitment to students and colleagues.

10. If you would like to know more about literacy development that evolves as a result of reading comic books, see pp. 46–60 of Krashen (1993). This fits into a broader perspective on light reading across the age levels, which adds to our literacy development. As Krashen states in this book, "Perhaps the most powerful way of encouraging children to read is by exposing them to light reading, a kind of reading that schools pretend does not exist, and a kind of reading that many children, for economic or ideological reasons, are deprived of. I suspect that light reading is the way nearly all of us learned to read" (pp. 48). Krashen's review of the literature about whole language studies (1999b) is worth your review, as is his review of sustained silent reading studies (1993). The report of Task Force on Racism and Bias in the Teaching of English, which provides guidelines for the construction of school literacy programs that are effective in promoting English language development, was published by National Council of Teachers of English (NCTE). This task force was led by Roseann Dueñas Gonzalez from the University of Arizona and the document, No. 16469–1450, is available at (www.ncte.org) or from NCTE, 1111 W. Kenyon Road, Urbana, IL 61801–1096.

11. For more critically grounded classroom activities, I refer you to Campbell (1996). Faltis & Wolf (1999) also provide good examples of critical practice within the classroom. Many who are cited in this chapter and in the reference section have activities to adopt and adapt to fit your own context. For other critically grounded activities, including math, I refer you to *Orillas* which focuses on those networking activities that affect social change, validate community traditions in the schools, and promote antiracist education and linguistic human rights. For information about how to participate, write to the co-founders of the project: Enid Figueroa, Kristin Brown, and Dennis Sayers at orillas-info@igc.org or 1801 SS Bar Ranch Road, Hornbrook, California, 96044, or call 530/475-0410.

chapter 5

Critical Pedagogy
Why in the World Does It Matter?

Kids matter. That's why. Our future matters. That's why. It is as simple as that. It also is something we all know. This is serious business we are talking about here. Students and teachers are hurting. We in education are a mirror of society that is more and more polarized.

Are poles really so bad? Let's relook and rethink poles. Aren't poles just opposite ways of thinking? Yes. Is diversity of thought bad? No. Would it really be so good if we all thought alike? I doubt it. I find it helpful to always think of the continuum that joins the poles. Aren't poles just an example of multiple voices and multiple ways of knowing along a continuum of thought? I think so. Are schools big enough for diversity? It's who we are.

We come from a tradition that assumed that *differences* were bad. Critical pedagogy teaches us to look again and to see again and to know in new ways that are a true reflection of today. Diversity of thought is good for schools and good for society.

Throughout this book, I have tried to show the many contradictions and changes we all are experiencing in our educational spaces. These contradictions and changes often frighten and offend us at first; they feel like polar opposites. We resist, we deny, we object. Critical pedagogy has helped me welcome these contradictions and changes. The poles no longer tear me apart. The poles are just a part of a larger picture that is our ever-increasing vibrant society.

The world is changing fast, and these societal changes are reflected every day in our schools. Every newspaper we pick up tells us again and again that what we are doing is not working. Historically, our schools are based on the needs of an agrarian society in which knowledge was controlled and transmitted by the schools. At the rate with which new knowledge and information are now being generated, it is impossible for even the very best teacher to be able to transmit it all. Students of the future need to be able to access new knowledge, critically reflect upon it, interpret it, and apply it in new ways. The changing world is dragging us (kicking and screaming, in some instances) into the world of a transformative model of education. The purpose of education is to transform society into a truly democratic environment for all. "Particularly is it true that a society which not only changes but which has the ideal of such change as will improve it, will have different standards and methods of education from one which aims simply at the perpetuation of its own custom" (Dewey, 1944; p. 81).

James Cummins has spoken repeatedly about the changing global realities, which he calls cultural, linguistic, scientific, technological, and ecological realities. In the new global realities, diversity of people and diversity of thought are the norm. This is the foundation for a thriving society; it is only when change ceases that societies begin to die. In a vibrant, dynamic society, diversity of thought enriches us all. More recently, this idea of global realities (Cummins & Sayers, 1995) has been expanded and now includes the idea of "existential realities," which encompasses the sense of fragility we experience in our relationship with the physical and social environment.

Cummins' idea of the new global realities certainly is affirmed in my own experiences. I rarely visit a school that is not multicultural, and many are multilingual. It appears to me that the mainstream is very multicultural. These changing global realities lead us to ask ourselves, What do students today need to know in order to thrive and flourish in the future? What are the needs of students and citizens of the twenty-first century?

STUDENTS OF THE TWENTY-FIRST CENTURY

We will need bilingual/biliterate students who love to read, can reflect critically, and live their lives with passion and action. We need collaborative, lifelong learners who are responsible for their own learning and understand that it comes from their lived experiences. We need students who can generate new knowledge and apply it in unknown ways. We need students who can write and rewrite their woild from a pluralistic perspective, students who can pose problems and solve problems with technology that stretches beyond our wildest thoughts. We need students who know how to access, interpret, and critically use new and emerging information. Above all, our students will need to be able to work in a multilingual and multicultural society. The students who will thrive socially and economically are those who bravely cross borders: cultural, linguistic, classist, sexist, and racial. We must begin with every teacher and every student and family in every school today. As a local teacher/grad student wrote at the end of an essay: *"My goal is to begin today."* I think that teacher has something to teach all of us.

I recently asked a group of teachers how they thought we should teach critically and effectively for the students of the twenty-first century. Their answers are worth sharing.

How to Teach for Students of the Twenty-First Century

Be passionate about your subject matter.
Know students and their backgrounds.
Involve the families as citizens of the classroom.
Allow students the freedom to explore and
time to sit and think.
Provide meaningful, practical, and relevant information.
Show students how to access and
generate new information.
Ask "why" a lot.
Make sure students see you reading.

The writing of this book has pushed me along my own unlearning curve. If anyone had told me 5 years ago that my study of critical pedagogy would bring me to this point, I never would have believed it. Even a year ago, I would not have believed it. However, by writing my own thoughts, I have discovered some of my own elusive answers. First, I seek my answers in the delicate balance between a caring heart and a critical eye. Second, I follow the path of action that is in that enlightened and precarious place between courage and patience. And third, this all takes time.

THE PEDAGOGY OF A CARING HEART AND CRITICAL EYES

It might seem at first that *caring* is poles apart from *critical*. Not for me. They are two parts of a new dynamic pedagogical whole. For me, the critical perspective and the centrality of caring come together under the framework of critical pedagogy. And no one is more surprised than I. I find strength in these seeming opposites. They fit in a new whole picture of schools. A complex picture. A diverse picture. A vibrant picture. And a very exciting and powerful new picture of the potential within all of us. Critical pedagogy has painted this new picture for me.

A Caring Heart

Why should kids care, if we don't? Caring counts. I would like to see teachers and learners enter into dialogue of some very fundamental human needs that are not being met in our schools, for example, love. It's true: Love trumps methods! I really have felt this for a long time, but I had to be patient until I had enough courage to say it. Critical pedagogy brought me here. I believe this is what McLaren is alluding to when he speaks of the *"teachable heart."*

I suggest that all of us in education should place our entire discussion of teaching and learning into a larger framework of caring. Nel Noddings (1992) has been a consistent voice in raising questions of ethics and values in schools. National educational journals are alive with the importance of caring. A national teacher of the year said it best, however, when referring to a former teacher who had turned his life around: "He put his hands on my shoulder that first day of class and it burned clear through to my heart" (Hanson, 1994, pp. A1, A11). As we live through these rapid social and demographic changes, I suspect that caring counts. Nowhere are these changes experienced more profoundly than in schools every day.

We come from various perspectives, experiences, and academic areas, but we all care about teaching and learning. In a safer world, that would be enough. However, in the social-cultural context of education of today, it is not enough. We also must care about ourselves, our colleagues, our students, and our communities. As Elam (1995) comments,

> In a more reasonable society, in a more perfect nation, in a world beyond ugly discriminations of gender, race, and class, our citizens would live in a convivial atmosphere of community. . . . That is why I worry a good deal about the soundness of the national mind and spirit. I worry about public voices that tout intolerance and narrow-mindedness. I worry about the politics of parsimony and isolation. . . . I still take comfort knowing that singular acts of care and compassion take place all the time and I hope for the day when these acts will become the very core of our culture. (p. A11)

Pedagogical caring must be balanced within the dialectic of a critical stance to meet the needs of teaching and learning for the twenty-first century. Critically reflecting on theory and practice and acting on our individual praxis are fundamental to critical pedagogy. A caring heart can be demonstrated in innumerable ways in the classroom and community, but a critically caring heart moves us along a critical path of unlearning.

The caring heart does not mean that we stop listening to the whispering of the juxtaposition: the critically reflective eye. Do not be fooled. Caring teachers and learners continue to look in the mirror, the classroom, and the community to discover their own path of unlearning. The caring heart and the critical eye often bring us to that enlightened and contradictory place where each begins to detect elusive answers.

A Critical Eye

Why should kids critically reflect if we don't? Teachers often talk about the importance of inquiry, of critical reflection, of active and engaged investigation, but if we don't, they won't.

The new century forces us to know in new ways, as Carole, a high school teacher, discovered:

> *A very profound learning experience shaped me as a teacher. When I first began my career, I had high "standards" for my students. It was to the point of being uncaring. After two years, I decided that love and compassion were more important than strict regulations. Today, the students and their outlook on life are more important than a rule. The irony is that as I begin to focus more on caring about the whole student and less about "standards" and "regulations," the students are learning more. I thought I was exchanging high "standards" for a little caring. The truth is the opposite: As I care more, the students learn more.*

Carole's experiences demonstrate just how confounding contradictions can be. Carole thought she used to have *high standards,* but as she began to critically reflect on her own practice, she has discovered that the students have higher standards for their own learning.

Thirty years ago a friend told me that teachers can hurt kids. I was shocked and did not (want to) believe it. Kim is a gentle, quiet teacher who critically reflects on her own theory and practice. She challenges herself to look again and see again, but even I was surprised when I read her paper. In this story she brings together the importance of a critical perspective, which can often lead us to a caring philosophical stance.

My first-grade teacher was a monster. (Kim wrote this with a black, felt-tipped pen, and underlined the word monster.*) She was mean. She liked to yell and threaten.*

One day someone turned out the lights while we were walking back to our classroom from music class. When we got back, she asked, "Who turned off the lights?" I remember how frightened and quiet we were.

"Nobody is leaving this room today until the person who did this confesses," she yelled at us. The bell rang to go home, and still no one confessed. We sat. We sat for what seemed to be a long time.

"I did it," I finally said. I was scared because I didn't think the teacher was going to let us go home. The other students were dismissed, and I had to stay in the room alone with the teacher. I remember her cold voice asking me why I had done it.

"I didn't. I just said it so we could go home," I said, as I started to cry.

She called me a liar. I remember the shame I felt. I will never forget that day.

My critical reflections of this experience have made me believe in the importance of caring in the classroom.

PEDAGOGY OF COURAGE AND PATIENCE

I also have started to notice that my years with students and my reading of all those critical theory books have led me to focus more and more on courage and patience. Once again, you may believe that courage and patience are poles apart. Not for me. They are part of that new pedagogical whole. Courage, sometimes. Patience other times. Only reflective action will help you decide which one when.

Just as teaching and learning form a dialectical union that propels our professional growth forward, so is the union of courage and patience fundamental to our pedagogy for the future. Daily, I feel the pull of courage and the counterpull of patience. Oftentimes we need to be as courageous as the context will allow. At other times, patience is our greatest ally: patience with ourselves, our colleagues, our context.

Presently, I am watching a district completely divided into two camps. I will call the two teams the White Sox and the Brown Sox. The school is divided, the community is divided, and all are being hurt. In the middle of this great battle is a young, beginning teacher, an ethnic minority who is being pummeled by the White Sox team. It appears to me that when the dust settles, the Board of Education will offer a contract for another year to the young teacher—a move that will outrage the White Sox and please the Brown Sox. I predict the young teacher will keep his job unless he leaves in complete discouragement, which probably is the hidden objective of the White Sox players. I watch the young teacher struggle to be courageous and defend himself; I watch him be patient with his adversaries. I can see the principal is walking a tight rope in her balance between courage and patience. They are in good company: "Paulo Freire lived the dialectic between patience and impatience. He had to be patient, impatiently. It was necessary to be impatient, patiently" (Gadotti, 1994, p. 47).

Candi is a teacher/grad student who works in a very coercive school setting. She understands that the school believes in transmission model education. Candi sees herself as a transformative educator. She has critically reflected and understands the barriers she faces. Candi also knows that her life is in this community, and she must find ways of living, learning, and teaching. She asked if we could use a class session to problem pose on her struggles with her environment. She shared honestly, as did her colleagues in the graduate class. At the end of this challenging session, they generated a plan based on the dialectical union of courage and patience. They decided Candi should commit to the following:

1. Be courageous enough to live her beliefs honestly.
2. Be courageous enough to invite her coteachers and administrators to her room when she would be doing a lesson design based on critical pedagogy.
3. Be patient enough to let her colleagues draw their own conclusions.
4. Be patient enough to listen and be courageous enough to repeat back adversarial comments.
5. Be courageous enough to accept the fact that she can't control others' beliefs; she can only live her own.

One year later Candi reports that her acceptance of the dialectical union of courage and patience has lead her to be a more joyful and rigorous teacher. She likes her colleagues and school better. Candi recognizes that she herself must be courageous and patient before she asks it of her students.

TIME. TIME. TIME.

All of this takes time. For example, the language of critical pedagogy takes time. The thoughts of critical pedagogy take time. Jonathan's literacy took time. A *teachable heart* takes time. Critically reflective practice takes time.

Challenging our own intellect takes time. Reading books on critical pedagogy takes time. Shifting our lesson designs takes time. Shifting our paradigm really takes time.

Time is more important than *coverage*. The elusive answers that are meaningful for me all seem to be grounded in issues of time. Traditionally, we have been driven by the pedagogy of *coverage*. We have to *cover* this now. We have to *cover* that next. However, *coverage* is not as important as learning. What good does it do to cover the material in the time allowed if students don't know it? As Jonathan said, "Even if I know how to spell *aboard* on Friday, I won't know it next Monday." Time traditionally controls teachers; I suggest that it ought to be the other way around. I also think that we, as educators, must continually reflect on coverage and time.

Why should we expect kids to take time if we don't? Recently, a former master's graduate called to tell me about a statistics class in her doctoral program. The professor, who was very intimidating, came to every class with 50 problems to cover. The frightened and frustrated students were not learning, but he continued to cover his 50 stat problems. The students endured several class periods. They sat quietly and passively and copied every number and every squiggle that he wrote on the board, but in all of this time, no one was *learning*. They were only *covering* his prescribed curriculum, 50 problems per class. The students were still too nervous to question him. Finally, in desperation, this former master's student raised her hand to ask for help in class.

> STUDENT: Professor, I did not understand the first problem. Would you please repeat your explanation?
> PROFESSOR: No, I have no time to repeat; I have 49 more problems to cover.
> STUDENT: Yes, but if I don't understand number one, it really doesn't matter what you do with the remaining 49.

This particular example screams of the dangers of the pedagogy of coverage. This professor thought he needed to *cover* 50 problems in the allotted time. Students don't need to *cover* 50 problems; they need to learn. We, as educators, need to reflect on our perspective of time. We feel controlled by time. However, in our own classes, we need to control the time.

The student had been patient and now was moving to courage. If only the professor had been courageous enough to be patient with his students' learning.

Jonathan's teacher felt that he had to *cover* spelling words every Monday; he felt that he had to test every Friday. Jonathan realized that the students needed to *know* the words—even on the next Monday.

I struggle with *coverage* and *time* in every class. I come in with my objectives, my gorgeous transparencies, my planned organization of the 3-hour block of time. The students keep interrupting me with meaningful questions. They keep relating their new knowledge from class to their own world. That darned transformative learning! It has even driven me to say, "Stop this learning; I want to teach!"

FROM BUTTERCUP TO POWER

Now here is the problem with all of these thoughts about a caring heart, a critical eye, and time: It causes us to confront ourselves; it takes away the blame-game; and it does it in the most surprising ways. In the introduction, I wrote that I would tell the story of how I was forced to confront my own fear of power. On the surface, this may appear to be a story about a horse. Do not be fooled. Until each of us owns our own power (negotiates our own identity), we cannot be a part of empowerment (negotiating identities with students).

It began so simply. Dawn told me to read Naomi Wolf (1993). Wolf hypothesizes that women's fear of horses is really a disguised fear of power. Her thesis is that preadolescent girls are fearless and courageous and often love horses. As they move through adolescence and seek to be more the way little boys want them to be, they develop a fear of horses—or fear of power.

When I read that, I slammed the book shut. One of my main myths exploded (Nieto, 1996). This was not a metaphor to me; this was my real world. I have lived a lot of my life on ranches. I grew up around horses and rode as a child. As a young adolescent, I became afraid of horses. This was also about the same time that I started noticing boys. I remember wishing they would think that I was "cute." Since that time, I rationalized my fear of horses this way: Horses are bigger than I, stronger than I, faster than I, and certainly smarter than I. I have consistently been in situations in which I had to make excuses about not wanting to go for a ride: "I'm busy"; or "I have to cook"; or "the kids need me." And my personal favorite: "Someone else can use my saddle." Sometimes I didn't succeed in talking my way out of a horseback ride. Invariably, long hours in a saddle followed, as I tried to hide my fear.

It seems that in life we sometimes bump into the right teacher when we are ready to learn. Apparently, I was there, and Wolf was the teacher. I stared out the window and set a new goal for myself: By the end of the summer, I would no longer be afraid of horses. I would be a horse-person.

In June we bought a horse named, Cowboy. I immediately changed his name to Buttercup. I was hoping that the change of name would make him gentle and me fearless. My goal was to go for one ride in the country alone by the end of the month. During each day of June, I went for short, easy rides with my husband, who did not understand my fear but who accepted and respected it. On the last day of the month, Buttercup and I went out for a 3-mile ride alone. It was not fun, but I did it.

July brought another goal: Buttercup and I were to race across the prairies with reckless abandon. I succeeded and can even do so without bouncing in the saddle and without my arms flailing in the wind—a prairie faux pas. Okay, it's true; I shouted with joy as I raced through the pasture.

My goal for August was not just to ride, but to be good at it. I wanted to actually be helpful when moving cows. I wanted to be able to chase a calf and bring it back to the herd. Goal met. I wanted to be able to move a herd of cows through a gate. Goal met. An angry bull can still bluff Buttercup and me, but this is not a story about angry bulls. This is a story about fear of power.

> At rare intervals, the most significant factors in determining the future occur in infinitesimal quantities on unique occasions (Mumsford, 1956).

TEACHERS TAUGHT ME, TOO

Throughout this book, I have written about the many things students taught me to learn and unlearn:

- Teaching is learning.
- If it doesn't matter to students, it doesn't matter.
- Change and contradictions are in every classroom.

In this chapter, I have told you how critical pedagogy comes together for me in new and surprising ways. Critical pedagogy has helped me understand that it is okay to be critical of processes that we don't philosophically support; it is okay to care a lot. Critical pedagogy has given me courage and taught me lessons of patience. And it is okay if all of this takes time.

Thirty years ago, when I started teaching, no one could have told me that teaching would bring me to this way of knowing. Education classes didn't teach me these important lessons; students did. We need to listen to and learn more from students. With changes happening so fast in our society today, I cannot imagine what students will teach me in the next 10 years. However, I am anxious to learn whatever it will be.

Now, a final word about teachers. The truth is that I have been blessed with the best, and I have learned from them.

What Teachers Taught Me

Caring counts.
Mem Fox

Learning should be rigorous and joyful.
Paulo Freire

Teachers are intellectuals.
Henry Giroux

Coercive relations of power don't work;
collaborative relations do.
James Cummins

Meaning matters.
Stephen Krashen

Good teachers and learners start with a teachable heart.
Peter McLaren

A Teams and B Teams are good for the A Team.
Tove Skutnabb-Kangas

It's fun to talk with a friend while we learn.
Lev Vygotsky

It's okay to learn while we teach.
The Benson Kids

NOW HERE IS THE POINT

Critical pedagogy is about hope! We all want it. Critical pedagogy led me to it. I started years ago reading those difficult, theoretical books. They made sense to me. I will never forget the first time I read McLaren (1989); I remember thinking: Yes. Yes. Yes. The first time I read Giroux (1988), I remember thinking: This room is vibrating. These books were like the kids I had been teaching. They were not theoretical pages. They were faces and hearts.

When I first began my study of critical pedagogy, I feared I would see too much, too critically. I feared I would lose "me" in those infuriating new words and old thoughts. However, the opposite has happened again. I'm not so sure these poles are all bad. Confounding contradictions. Critical pedagogy has given me hope.

Why does critical pedagogy matter? It matters because J.J. matters.

> *Steve, a friend who is actively involved within his community, told me this story about a young African American teenage boy, J.J. Steve has a special interest in teenage boys who are lost and adrift. J.J. is almost a stereotype of a marginalized and angry young black man. He comes from an economically disadvantaged family; his father abandoned them many years ago. J.J.'s mom is working hard, for long hours, with low pay. Gangs, drugs, and fast money were becoming more and more appealing to J.J.*
>
> *On this particular occasion, J.J. was in trouble (again) at school, and Steve was called in to talk with him. Steve did not talk. He listened.*
>
> *"You know what you got, and I ain't got? Hope. You got it. I want it," J.J. yelled at Steve.*

Steve and J.J. come from worlds that are poles apart. They are breaking those traditional barriers of race and class. They come together in a safe and social environment (the park) every week. This does not cost anyone anything. Steve and J.J. have committed their time, their courage, and their patience. They care about each other. They critically reflect on ways of generating hope in J.J.'s life. Their story is a powerful mandate for what each of us can do, must do. The kids and the future matter. (See Note 1.) "And it is through changing the present that we make the future" (Freire, as cited in Gadotti, 1994, p. 148).

TO MAKE A DIFFERENCE

One of the most important lessons that I have ever learned from educators is always to leave them with one final method, something that they can do tomorrow in their own schools and communities. This, then, is my last activity. Critical pedagogy has been assigned many esoteric and abstract meanings, most of which have enriched my life as a teacher and a learner. This critical perspective will continue to drive my own relearning and unlearning.

Most of us went into education "to make a difference." For many, this phase soon became just another reason to be cynical. Critical pedagogy has not only taken this cynicism away from me, it has given me hope. It has led me to believe that I really can make a difference. Conscientization. Self- and social transformation. Empowerment. Problem posing. Praxis. Action. They are no longer words to learn; they are no longer things I *do*; now they are ideas I strive to *live* every day.

Bob

Recently, I have been hearing a story about a particular teacher. In fact, I have heard four different versions of the same story. I will tell the story the way I heard it the first time, although I have since discovered what I assume to be the source of the original story (Bridges, 1993). It seems this teacher decided she would make one small change in her teaching. It would not cost anything. She would not have to ask permission from an administrator. It would not take much of her time. She would not have to go to meetings at night, write a document, or seek the school board's permission. It was just one small change. Maybe, just maybe, she could make a difference.

> *She went to a local trophy shop and ordered blue ribbons that said, I Make a Difference. When the ribbons arrived, she reflected seriously on each of her 30 students. Each student was special and had made unique contributions to the class and to her life. She knew she had learned from every one. Reflection. But she had never taken the time to tell the students. Action. She decided to tell each student in front of the class what she felt was each one's unique contribution to the class and how each one had enriched her life.*
>
> *On the Blue Ribbon Day, she took her time as she expressed her appreciation for each student's distinctive gift to the class and to her life. The students were silent as she spoke and as she pinned a blue ribbon on each shirt right above the heart. She was astounded at the*

reaction of her students. Some of them had never heard such sincere and honest praise. Many tears and shy smiles expressed their feelings. After the blue ribbon ceremony, she told the class that they had to leave with two more ribbons so they, too, could express appreciation to someone in their life.

Eventually, one of these blue ribbons made its way to a young junior executive, Bob, at a large company. He agonized over what he should do with his. He was the supervisor for many employees. He went through each name, and finally decided he had to give the blue ribbon to his boss, Paul Long, who had a reputation for being unapproachable, elitist, and grumpy. Everyone, including the junior executives, avoided him.

With butterflies in his stomach, Bob knocked on the office door of the CEO.

"Come in," Mr. Long grumbled. It was clear to Bob that his boss was distracted, busy, and did not want to be disturbed.

"Mr. Long, I am here to tell you that I appreciate you as the visionary leader of this company. Without your forethought and planning, we would never be able to succeed in this business. You make a difference in my life, and you make a valuable contribution in this community. I would like permission to reach across your desk and pin a blue ribbon on your shirt." Bob pinned the I Make a Difference blue ribbon on the pocket of his CEO.

Paul was speechless. He finally managed to mumble his appreciation.

"Mr. Long, here is another blue ribbon. You need to pin it on someone who has made a difference in your life," Bob said as he placed a second blue ribbon on Paul's large desk.

Bob left the office with a sense that he had chosen the right person, and Paul Long went home to his family. He did not mention what had happened at work that day. His family did not notice his silence, because it was his custom to eat dinner and then to talk on the phone in his den. However, tonight Paul was thinking about who should receive his blue ribbon. He finally decided.

He walked down the hallway to his son's bedroom. His son, Paul, Jr, was 17 years old.

"Son, I know that I often don't speak honestly with you. I know that I am often too busy. But, I want you to know that you make all the difference in my life." As he said this, Paul, Sr, reached over and pinned the I Make a Difference blue ribbon on Paul, Jr.

His son began to cry and was soon sobbing. His head hung, and his shoulders were heaving up and down with each sob.

"Son, what is the matter?" his dad said.

"Dad, no one ever told me that I make a difference. I had been planning on committing suicide tomorrow, and now I don't have to do it."

What good is this story if we don't turn it into action? Critical pedagogy has taught me that my actions can make a difference. Beginning this semester, I will award an *I Make a Difference* blue ribbon to each of my grad students/teachers. I will make time to tell my students how they make a difference in the community of our classroom and in my life. And I will give each of them more blue ribbons that they can pass on to their students or others in their life. Dawn will be doing the same thing with her new group of fourth graders.

Won't you join us? I will begin to collect all the stories that demonstrate how each of us can make a difference. Without studying critical pedagogy for years, I would never have had the courage to do this, nor the patience to wait for the stories of power, love, and caring.

Roxanne

Here is one of those stories: Roxanne is an English-dominant teacher and grad student who is studying bilingual and multilingual education for the first time. After reading Cummins (1989), she shared her feelings with the class.

"I cannot solve the whole world's problems, but I can start with myself and the students in my class," she matter-of-factly told her colleagues. "After reading Empowering Language Minority Students, *I have some thoughts about what I can do."*

What I can do:

- I will not make a judgment about the students based on any test (language or psychological) that is not in the language of the students.
- I will not label. If English is the language of the classroom, and they are not yet able to learn in English, I will find them help. I will not make assumptions about "language difficulties" for bilingual students who are in the process of acquiring English.
- I will encourage all students to speak in their own language.

- I will respect the culture of each student by encouraging students to share and write about their families and traditions.
- I will post assignments in multiple languages all around the classroom.
- I will invite the students' parents to the classroom to read and to share with us.
- I will hang signs around the school in the languages of the students.
- I will encourage all students to speak and to learn in their primary language.
- I will invite community members to my class.
- And, most importantly, I will provide books in the languages of the students.

I have probably read Cummins (1989) more times than I can count, but I have to thank Roxanne for forcing me to turn theory into practice—an ongoing process for all of us. Roxanne discovered how she can make a difference. She named, she reflected critically, and, she acted, which many would say is a good definition of critical pedagogy.

How are you doing critical pedagogy?

LOOKING AHEAD FOR MORE ELUSIVE ANSWERS

"Life," said Izzy, "is a series of strange and seemingly pointless stories. Meaning is derived from a relationship of story, storyteller, and listener. By far the hardest task is that of the listener." (Kaminsky, 1991, p. 84, as cited in Vallance, 1995)

You are the listener. Why in the world does critical pedagogy matter to you? This book is filled with my stories, my ideas, my perspective, my experiences, my biases, my voice. However, I think this book would be more valuable if you would read and write *with* me. Reading is one way of acquiring knowledge. Writing is one way of inquiring into your own knowledge. Write your stories, your ideas, your perspective, your experiences, your biases, your voice, and your ways of knowing. Critical pedagogy has taught me to be a listener and a storyteller. I encourage you to listen and tell your stories.

How should I end this book? Of course, with a beginning: Yours! Why should we expect kids to write if we don't?

NOTE

1. J.J. is a living example of what Herb Kohl (1998) finds in his four decades of teaching and learning. There is hope for education in the most surprising places and times and with students who have previously had little hope. This is very much what I have learned from students.

Bibliography

Ada, A. F. (1988a). Creative reading: A relevant methodology for language minority children. In L. M. Malave (Ed.), *NABE '87. Theory, research and application: Selected papers* (pp. 97-111). Buffalo: State University of New York Press.

Ada, A. F. (1988b). The Pájaro Valley experience: Working with Spanish-speaking parents to develop children's reading and writing skills in the home through the use of children's literature. In T. Skutnabb-Kangas & J. Cummins (Eds.), *Minority education: From shame to struggle* (pp. 223-238). Philadelphia, PA: Multilingual Matters.

Ada, A. F. (1988, March 20). Honoring the life and legacy of Paulo Freire. Symposium conducted at Teachers of English to Speakers of Other Languages (TESOL) '98, Seattle, WA.

Auerbach, E. (1995a). Critical issues: Deconstructing the discourse of strengths in family literacy. *JRB: A Journal of Literacy, 27,* pp. 643-661.

Auerbach, E. (1995b). From deficit to strength: Changing perspectives on family literacy. In G. Weinstein-Shr & E. Quintero (Eds.), *Immigrant learners and their families* (pp. 59-62). McHenry, IL: Center for Applied Linguistics and Delta Systems.

August, D., & Hakuta, K. (Eds.). (1997). *Improving schooling for language-minority children: A research agenda* (pp. 17-32). Washington, D.C.: National Academy Press.

Bancroft, A. (1995, March 28). 20 Years of affirmative action: Still no parity. *The Modesto Bee,* p. A8.

Bigelow, G., Christensen, L., Karp, S., Miner, B., & Peterson, B. (1994). *Rethinking our classrooms: Teaching for equity and justice.* Milwaukee, WI: Rethinking Schools, Ltd.

Berliner D., & Biddle, B. (1995). *The manufactured crisis: Myths, fraud, and the attack on America's public schools.* New York: Addison Wesley Longman, Inc.

Blanck, G. (1990). Vygotsky: The man and his cause. In L. Moll (Ed.), *Vygotsky and education* (pp. 31-58). New York: Cambridge University Press.

Bowles, S., & Gintis, H. (1976). *Schooling in capitalist America.* New York: Basic Books.

Bridges, H. (1993). Who you are makes a difference. In J. Canfield & M. V. Hanson (Eds.), *Chicken soup for the soul* (pp.19-21). Deerfield Beach, FL: Health Communications.

Campbell, D. (1996). *Choosing democracy: A practical guide to multicultural education.* Englewood Cliffs, NJ: Prentice-Hall, Inc.

Canfield, J., & Hanson, M. V. (Eds.). (1993). *Chicken soup for the soul*. Deerfield Beach, FL: Health Communications.

Carnes, J. (1995, Spring). Home was a horse stall. *Teaching Tolerance, 50-57*.

Cortés, C. (Ed.). (1986). *The education of language minority students: A contextual interaction model*. Los Angeles: Evaluation, Dissemination, and Assessment Center, California State University.

Crawford, J. (1999). *Bilingual education: History, politics, theory, and practice*. (4th ed.). Los Angeles: Bilingual Education Services, Inc.

Cremin, L. (1964). *The transformation of the school*. New York: Vantage Books.

Csikszentmihalyi, M. (1997). *Finding flow: The psychology of engagement in everyday life*. NY: Basic Books.

Cummins, J. (1989). *Empowering minority students*. Sacramento: California Association for Bilingual Education.

Cummins, J. (1994). The socioacademic achievement model in the context of coercive and collaborative relations of power. In R. DeVillar, C. Faltis, & J. Cummins (Eds.), *Cultural diversity in schools: From rhetoric to practice* (pp. 363-390). Albany: State University of New York Press.

Cummins, J., & Sayers, D. (1995). *Brave new schools: Challenging cultural illiteracy*. New York: St. Martin's Press.

Cummins, J. (1996). *Negotiating identities: Education for empowerment in a diverse society*. Sacramento: California Association of Bilingual Education.

Cummins, J. (1998, March 20). *Honoring the life and legacy of Paulo Freire*. Symposium conducted at Teachers of English to Speakers of Other Languages (TESOL)'98, Seattle, WA.

DeMarrais, K.B., & LeCompte, M.D. (1999). *The way schools work: A sociological analysis of education*. New York: Addison Wesley Longman, Inc.

Dewey, J. (1944). *Democracy and education*. New York: Free Press, a Division of Simon & Shuster Inc.

Dewey, J. (1947). *Experience and education*. NY: Macmillan Company.

Edelsky, C. (1991). *With literacy and justice for all: Rethinking the social in language and education*. Bristol, PA: Falmer Press.

Elam, R. (1995, March 3). Voices of reason and compassion. *The Modesto Bee*, p. A11.

Fader, D. N., & McNeil, E. B. (1966). *Hooked on books: Program & proof*. New York: Berkley Medallion Books.

Faltis, C. (1990). Freirian and Vygotskian perspective. *Foreign Language Annals, 23*(2), 117-126.

Faltis, C., & Wolfe, P. (1999). *So much to say: Adolescents, bilingualism and ESL in the secondary school*. New York: Teachers College Press.

Farr, R., and Tone, B. (1994). *Portfolio and performance assessment: Helping students evaluate their progress as readers and writers*. Fort Worth, TX: Harcourt Brace College Publishers.

Field, R. (1996). *John Dewey. Internet encyclopedia of philosophy*. [On-line]. Available: http://www.wtm.edu/research/iep/d/dewey.htm

Fishman, J. (1976). *Bilingual education: An international sociological perspective*. Rowley, MA: Newbury House.

Fishman, J. (1991). *Reversing language shift*. Clevedon, England: Multilingual Matters.

Fishman, S., and McCarthy, L. (1998). John Dewey and the challenge of classroom practice. New York: Teachers College Press.

Fleischer, C., & Schaafsma, D. (Eds.). (1998). *Literacy and democracy: Teacher research and composition studies in pursuit of habitable spaces*. Urbana, IL: National Council of Teachers of English.

Flood, J., Lapp, D., Tinajero, J., & Hurley, S. (1996, December/1997 January). Literacy instruction for students acquiring English: Moving beyond the immersion debate. *The Reading Teacher, 50*(4), 356-358.

Fox, M. (1993). *Radical reflections: Passionate opinions on teaching, learning, and living.* San Diego, CA: Hartcourt Brace & Company.

Freeman, Y., & Freeman, D. (1992). *Whole language for second language learners.* Portsmouth, NH: Heinemann.

Freeman, Y., & Freeman, D. (1994). *Between worlds: Access to second language acquisition.* Portsmouth, NH: Heinemann.

Freeman, Y., & Freeman, D. (1998). *ESL/EFL Teaching: Principles for success.* Portsmouth, NH: Heinemann.

Freire, P. (1974). *Pedagogy of the oppressed.* New York: Seabury Press.

Freire, P. (1993, February 4). *Teaching and learning.* Paper presented at the California Association for Bilingual Education, Anaheim, CA.

Freire, P. (1994). *The pedagogy of hope: Reliving pedagogy of the oppressed.* New York: Continuum Publishing Group.

Freire, P., & Macedo, D. (1987). *Literacy: Reading the word and the world.* South Hadley, MA: Bergin & Garvey.

Gadotti, M. (1994). *Reading Paulo Freire: His Life and Work.* Albany: State University of New York Press.

Galtung, J. (1980). *The true worlds: A transactional perspective.* New York: The Free Press.

García, H. S. (1993). Shifting the paradigms of education and language policy: Implications for language minority children. *The Journal of Educational Issues of Language Minority Students, 12*, 1-6.

Gee, J. (1996). *Social linguistics and literacies: Ideology in discourses.* Bristol, PA: Falmer Press.

Gee, J. (1992). *The social mind: Language, ideology, and social practice.* New York: Bergin and Garvey.

Giroux, H. (1988). *Teachers as intellectuals: Toward a critical pedagogy of learning.* South Hadley, MA: Bergin & Garvey.

Glass ceiling intact. (1995, March 16). *The Sacramento Bee,* pp. A1, A24.

Goodman, K. (1998). *In defense of good teaching: What teachers need to know about the "reading wars."* York, ME: Stenhouse Publishers.

Goldberg, M. (1995). Portrait of John Goodlad. *Educational Leadership, 52*(6), 82-85.

Gramsci, A. (1971). *Selections from the prison notebooks.* London, England: Lawrence & Wishart.

Greene, M. (1998, April 17). *Honoring the legacy of Paulo Freire.* Symposium conducted at a meeting of American Educational Research Association (AERA), San Diego, CA.

Hanson, D. (1994, August 27). Caring spells career success for teacher. *The Turlock Journal,* pp. A1, A11.

Harris, T., & Hodges, R. (Eds.). (1995). *The literacy dictionary: The vocabulary of reading and writing.* Newark, DE: International Reading Association.

Hasselstrom, L. (1987). *Winkbreak: A woman rancher on the Northern plains.* Berkeley, CA: Barn Owl Books.

Horton, M., & Freire, P. (1990). *We make the road by walking: Conversations on education and social change.* Philadelphia: Temple University Press.

Jasso, A., & Jasso, R. (1995). Critical pedagogy: Not a method, but a way of life. In J. Frederickson (Ed.), *Reclaiming our voices: Bilingual education, critical pedagogy and praxis* (pp. 253-259). Ontario, CA: California Association for Bilingual Education.

Johnson, D., & Johnson, R. (1987). Research shows the benefits of adult cooperation. *Educational Leadership, 45*(3), 27–30.

Kagan, S. (1990). *Cooperative learning: Resources for teachers.* Riverside: Printing and Repographics, University of California, Riverside.

Kanpol, B. (1994). *Critical pedagogy: An introduction.* Westport, CT: Bergin & Garvey.

Kohl, H. (1994). *I won't learn from you: And other thoughts on creative maladjustment.* New York: The New Press.

Kohl, H. (1998). *The discipline of hope: Learning from a lifetime of teaching.* NY: Simon & Schuster.

Kozulin, A. (Ed.). (1986). Vygtosky in context. In *L. S. Vygotsky: Thought and language* (pp. xi-lvi). Cambridge, MA: MIT Press.

Krashen, S. (1994, October 24). *Second language acquisition.* Syposium for Multidistrict Trainer of Trainer's Institute, San Joaquín County Office of Education, Stockton, CA.

Krashen, S. (1993). *The power of reading: Insights from the research.* Englewood, CO: Libraries Unlimited, Inc.

Krashen, S. (1996). *Under attack: The case against bilingual education.* Culver City, CA: Language Education Associates.

Krashen, S. (Summer/Fall 1998). Is 180 days enough? *Bilingual Basics, 1*(2), 1–4.

Krashen, S. (1998, August). Why did California voters pass Prop 227? They thought they were voting for English. *TABE Newsletter, Tucson Association for Bilingual Education,* 3–4.

Krashen, S. (1998, November/December). Has whole language failed? *ESL Magazine, 1*(6), pp. 8–10.

Krashen, S. (1999a). *Condemned without a trial: Bogus arguments against bilingual education.* Westport, CT: Heinemann.

Krashen, S. (1999b). *Three arguments against whole language and why they are wrong.* Westport, CT: Heinemann.

Krashen, S., Tse, L., & McQuillan, J. (1998). *Heritage language development.* Culver City, CA: Language Education Associates.

Kuhn, T. (1970). *The structure of scientific revolutions.* Chicago, IL: University of Chicago Press.

Lankshear, C., & McLaren, P. (Eds.). (1993). *Critical literacy: Politics, praxis, and the postmodern.* Albany: State University of New York Press.

Leistyna, P., Woodrum, A., & Sherblom, S. (Eds.). (1996). Breaking free: The transformative power of critical pedagogy. Cambridge, MA: *Harvard Educational Review.*

Levine, D., Lowe, R., Peterson, B., and Tenorio, R. (Eds.). (1995). Rethinking schools: An agenda for change. New York: The New Press.

Lieberman, A. (1986). Collaborative research: Working with, not working on. *Educational Leadership, 43*(5), 29–31.

Lindfors, J. (1982). Exploring in and through language. In M. A. Clarke & J. Handscombe (Eds.), *On TESOL '82: Pacific perspectives on language learning and teaching.* Washington, DC: Teachers of English to Speakers of Other Languages.

Macedo, D. (Ed.). (1994). *Literacies of power.* Boulder, CO: Westview Press.

McCaleb, S. P. (1994). *Building communities of learners.* New York: St. Martin's Press.

McLaren, P. (1998). *Life in schools: An introduction to critical pedagogy in the foundations of education* (3rd ed.). NY: Longman.

McLaren, P. (1994). Critical pedagogy: Constructing an arch of social dreaming and a doorway to hope. In L. Erwin & D. MacLennan (Eds.), *Sociology of education in Canada: Critical perspectives on theory, research & practice* (pp. 137-160). Toronto: Copp Clark Longman.

McLaren, P. (1998, Summer). Che: The pedagogy of Che Guevara: Critical pedagogy and globalization thirty years after Che. *Cultural Circles, 3,* 29-103.

McQuillan, J. (1998a). Is 99% failure a "success"?: Orange Unified's English Immersion Program. *The Multilingual Educator, 21*(7), p. 11. (Availiable: www.bilingualeducation.org)

McQuillan, J. (1998b). *The literacy crisis: False claims, real solutions*. Portsmouth, NH: Heinemann.

Moares, M. (1996). Bilingual education: A dialogue with the Bakhtin circle. Albany, NY: State University of New York Press.

Moffett, J. (1989). Censorship and spiritual education. *English Education, 21,* 70-87.

Moll, L. (Ed.). (1990). *Vygotsky in education: Instructional implications and applications of sociohistorical psychology*. New York: Cambridge University Press.

Moll, L., & Greenberg, J. (1990). Creating zones of possibilities: Combing social contexts for instruction. In L.C. Moll (Ed.), *Vygotsky and education* (pp. 319-348). NY: Cambridge University Press.

Morrow, L. (Ed.). (1995). *Family literacy: Connections in schools and communities*. Newark, DE: International Reading Association.

Mumsford, L. (1956). *The transformations of man*. NY: Harper.

Mungazi, D. (1993). *Educational policy and national character: Africa, Japan, the United States, and the Soviet Union*. Wesport, CT: Greenwood Press.

Naysmith, J. (1987). English as imperialism. *Language Issues, 1*(2), 3-5.

Neuman, S., Caperelli, B., & Kee, C. (1998, November). Literacy learning, a family matter. *The Reading Teacher, 52*(3), 244-252.

Newman, J. (1998). *America's teachers: An introduction to education*. New York: Longman Publishers.

Nieto, S. (1996). *Affirming diversity: The sociopolitical context of multicultural education*. White Plains, NY: Longman Publishers USA.

Noddings, N. (1992). *The challenge to care in schools: An alternative approach to education*. New York: Teachers College Press.

Norris, K. (1993). *Dakota: A spiritual geography*. NY: Ticknor & Fields.

Oakes, J. (1985). *Keeping track: How schools structure inequality*. New Haven, CT: Yale University Press.

O'Cadiz, M., Lindquist Wong, P., & Torres, C. (1998). *Education and Democracy: Paulo Freire, social movements, and educational reform in Sao Paulo*. Boulder, CO: Westview Press.

Oyler, C. (1996). *Making room for students: Sharing teacher authority in Room 104*. New York: Teachers College, Columbia University.

Palincsar, A. (1996). Language-minority students: Instructional issues in school cultures and classroom social systems. *The Elementary School Journal, 96*(3), 221-226.

Palmer, P. (1998). *The courage to teach: Exploring the inner landscape of a teacher's life*. San Francisco, CA: Jossey-Bass Publishers.

Patterson, L., Baldwin, S., Gonzales, R., Guadarrama, I., Keith, L., & McArthur, K. (1998). *Claiming our ignorance and making new friends: Case studies in collaborative family inquiry*. A paper presented at 48th Annual Meeting of the National Reading Conference, Austin, TX.

Pattanayak, D. (1969). *Aspects of applied linguistics*. London: Asia Publishing House.

Peller, G. (1987). Reason and the mob: The politics of representation. *Tikkun, 2*(3), 28-95.

Pennycook, A. (1994). *The cultural politics of English as an international language*. New York: Addison Wesley Longman, Inc.

Phillipson, R. (1992). *Linguistic imperialism*. Oxford: Oxford University Press.

Poplin, M. & Weeres, J. (1992). *Voices from the inside: A report on schooling from inside the classroom*. Claremont, CA: The Institute for Education in Transformation at the Claremont Graduate School.

Pervil, S. (Ed.). (1998, October). *Primary voices: Democracy in the classroom, 7(2).*

Putney, L. G. (1993). *A descriptive study of sheltered social studies for second language learners.* Unpublished Master's thesis, California State University, Stanislaus, Turlock.

Putney, L. G., Green, J. L., Dixon, C. N., Duran, R., & Yeager, B. (1999). Consequential progressions: Exploring collective-individual development in a bilingual classroom. In C. D. Lee & P. Smagorinsky (Eds.), *Constructing meaning through collaborative inquiry: Vygotskian perspectives on literacy research.* New York: Cambridge University Press.

Quindlen, A. (1998). *How reading changed my life.* NY: Ballantine Publishing Group.

Rinvolucri, M. (1990). *The confidence book.* White Plains, NY: Longman Publishers, USA.

Rinvolucri, M. (1995). *Dictation: New methods, new possibilities.* England: Cambridge University Press.

Sacks, C.H., & Mergendoller, J.R. (1997). The relationship between teachers' theoretical orientation toward reading and student outcomes in kindergarten children with different initial reading abilities. *American Educational Research Journal, 34(4),* 721–739.

Scott-Maxwell, F. (1983). *The measure of my days.* NY: Penguin Books.

Skutnabb-Kangas, T. (1993, February 10). *Problem posing within the community.* Symposium for Graduate Students, California State University, Stanislaus, Turlock, CA.

Skutnabb-Kangas, T. (1998, March 20). *The politics of (ESL in) multilingual education. Languages, culture, power, and liberation.* Paper presented at the meeting of Teachers of English to Speakers of Other Languages (TESOL) 1998, Seattle, WA.

Skutnabb-Kangas, T. (in press, 2000). *Linguistic genocide in education: Or worldwide diversity and human rights.* Mahwah, NJ: Lawrence Erlbaum Associates.

Skutnabb-Kangas, T., & Cummins, J. (1988). Concluding remarks: Language for empowerment. In T. Skutnabb-Kangas & J. Cummins (Eds.), *Minority education: From shame to struggle* (pp. 390–394). Philadelphia, PA: Multilingual Matters.

Skutnabb-Kangas, T., & Phillipson, R. (1998). *Wanted! Linguistic human rights.* Rolig Papir 44. Roskilde Universitetscenter, Denmark.

Smith, N. J. (1995). Making the invisible visible: Critical pedagogy as a viable means of educating children. In J. Frederickson (Ed.), *Reclaiming our voices: Bilingual education, critical pedagogy & praxis* (pp. 241–252). Ontario, CA: California Association for Bilingual Education.

Taylor, D. (1998). *Beginning to read and the spin doctors of science: The political campaign to change America's mind about how children learn to read.* Urbana, Il: National Council of Teachers of English.

Tollefson, J. (1991). *Planning language, planning inequality: Language policy in the community.* Harlow, England: Longman.

Vallance, E. (1995). The public curriculum of orderly images. *Educational Researcher, 24(2),* 4–13.

Vygotsky, L. S. (1962). *Thought and language* (E. Hanfmann & G. Vakar, Trans.). Cambridge, MA: MIT Press.

Vygotsky, L. S. (1978). *Mind in society: The development of higher psychological processes.* Cambridge, MA: Harvard University Press.

Wallas, G. (1926). *The art of thought.* New York: Harcourt, Brace and Company.

Wallerstein, N. (1983). *Language and culture in conflict: Problem-posing in the ESL classroom.* New York: Addison-Wesley Publishing Company, Inc.

Westbrook, R. (1991). *John Dewey and American democracy.* Ithica, New York: Cornell University Press.

Wheatley, M. (1992). *Leadership and the new science.* San Francisco, CA: Barrett-Kohler Publishers.

Wink, J. (1991). *The emergence of the framework for intervention in bilingual education.* Unpublished doctoral dissertation, Texas A&M University, College Station, TX.

Wink, J. (Fall 1991). Immersion confusion. *TESOL Matters, 1,* 6.

Wink, J., & Almanzo, M. (1995). Critical pedagogy: A lens through which we see. In J. Frederickson (Ed.), *Reclaiming our voices: Bilingual education, critical pedagogy & praxis* (pp. 210-223). Ontario, CA: California Association for Bilingual Education.

Wink, J., Putney, L., & Bravo-Lawrence, I. (1994, September/October). Introduction: La voz de Vygotsky. *CABE Newsletter, 17*(2), 10-11, 13-14.

Wink, J., Putney, L., & Bravo-Lawrence, I. (1994, November/December). Lev Vygotsky: Who in the world was he? *CABE Newsletter, 17*(3), 8-9, 19-20.

Wink, J., Putney, L., & Bravo-Lawrence, I. (1995, January/February). Socioculturally learning: What in the world does it mean? *CABE Newsletter, 17*(4), 8-9, 22.

Wink, J., Putney, L., & Bravo-Lawrence, I. (1995, March/April). The zone of proximal development: How in the world do we create it? *CABE Newsletter, 17*(5), 12-13, 24.

Wink, J., Putney, L., & Bravo-Lawrence, I. (1995, May/June). Creating community a la Lev: Why in the world does it matter? *CABE Newsletter, 17*(6), 11, 22-23.

Wink, J., & Swanson, P. (1993, December). Rethinking lesson designs. *CSU, Stanislaus School of Education Journal, 10*(1), 30-35.

Wink, J., & Wu, Y. (1993, September/October). An introduction to critical pedagogy and the classroom teacher. *CABE Newsletter, 16*(2), 11-12.

Wink, J., & Wu, Y. (1993, November/December). Critical pedagogy: What in the world is it? *CABE Newsletter, 16*(3), 5, 24-26.

Wink, J., & Wu, Y. (1994, January/February). Critical pedagogy: Where in the world did it come from? *CABE Newsletter, 16*(4), 5, 18-19, 21, 23.

Wink, J., & Wu, Y. (1994, March/April). Critical pedagogy: How in the world do you do it? *CABE Newsletter, 16*(5), 25, 28, 30.

Wink, J., & Wu, Y. (1994, May/June). Critical pedagogy: Why in the world does it matter? *CABE Newsletter, 16*(6), 12-13, 21.

Wink, J., & Wink Moran, D. (forthcoming, 2000). Dual language models of education. In R. Phillipson (Ed.), *Rights to language: Equity, power, and education.* Mahwah, NJ: Lawrence Erlbaum Associates.

Wolf, N. (1993). *Fire with fire: The new female power and how it will change the 21st century.* London England: Random House.

Credits

Text credits in order of occurrence:

P. 33, from "Making the Invisible Visible: Critical Pedagogy as a Viable Means of Educating Children," by N.J. Smith, 1995, in *Reclaiming Our Voices: Bilingual Education, Critical Pedagogy, & Praxis* (pp. 241-252) Ontario, CA: California Association for Bilingual Education.

P. 36, from *Life in Schools: An Introduction to Critical Pedagogy in the Foundations of Education* (p. 174), by P. McLaren, 1998, White Plains, NY: Longman. Copyright 1989 by Longman Publishers USA. Reprinted with permission.

P. 74, from *The Pedagogy of Hope: Reliving Pedagogy of the Oppressed,* by P. Freire, 1994, New York: Continuum Publishing Group. Copyright 1994 by the Continuum Publishing Group. Reprinted with permission.

P. 80, from *Literacy: Reading the Word and the World* (pp. 124-125), by P. Freire and D. Macedo, 1987, South Hadley, MA: Bergin & Garvey. Reprinted with permission of Greenwood Publishing Group, Inc., Westport, CT. Copyright 1987.

P. 85-86, from *Social Linguistics and Literacies: Ideology in Discourses* (p. 31), by J. Gee, 1990, Bristol, PA: Falmer Press. Copyright 1990 by the Falmer Press. Reprinted with permission.

P. 103, from "Portrait of John Goodlad," by M. Goldberg, 1995, *Educational Leadership, 52,* p. 85. Copyright 1995 by the Association for Supervision and Curriculum Development. Reprinted with permission.

P. 110, from *Empowering Minority Students* (p. 59), by J. Cummins, 1989, Sacramento, CA: California Association for Bilingual Education.

P. 111, from *Minority Education: From Shame to Struggle* (p. 390), by T. Skutnabb-Kangas and J. Cummins, 1988, Philadelphia, PA: Multilingual Matters. Copyright 1988 by Multilingual Matters. Reprinted by permission.

P. 119, from *Reading Paulo Freire: His Life and Work* (p. 6), by M. Gadotti (1994), Albany: State University of New York Press. Copyright 1994 by State University of New York Press. Reprinted with permission.

P. 135, from "Shifting the Paradigms of Education and Language Policy: Implications for Language Minority Children," by H. S. Garcia, 1993, *The Journal of Educational Issues of Language Minority Students, 12,* p. 4. Copyright 1993 by Boise State University. Reprinted with permission.

P. 170, from "Caring Spells Career Success for the Teacher," by D. Hanson, August 27, 1994, *The Turlock Journal,* pp. A1-A16. Copyright 1994 by Turlock Journals. Reprinted with permission.

P. 170, from "Voices of Reason and Compassion," by R. Elam, March 3, 1995, *The Modesto Bee,* p. A11. Copyright 1995 by The Modesto Bee. Reprinted with permission.

P. 182, from "The Public Curriculum of Orderly Images," by E. Vallance, 1995, *Educational Researcher, 24* (2), p. 84. Copyright 1995 by the American Educational Research Association. Reprinted with permission.

Index